CW00457807

Throwing Parties: A Guide to Being a Great Host

By Luke Johnson
and Graeme Boyd

Text © Luke Johnson and Graeme Boyd 2024 All rights reserved

First published in Great Britain by John Wilkes Publishing in
partnership with Risk Capital Publishing 2024
Printed in Latvia by Livonia Print
Designed, typeset and front cover by Alan Craig ALN Design
Picture research by Graeme Boyd

Font: Minion Pro 13pt
British Library Cataloguing-in-Publication Data

A catalogue record is available from the British Library
ISBN 978-1-7390926-0-3

Foreword by Peter York

Contents

Foreword

"Mmmmmmmmmmmmmmmm" was how the genius New York essayist/ satirist and later novelist Tom Wolfe described guests' reactions to the canapés – "Little Roquefort cheese morsels rolled in crushed nuts" – at Leonard and Felicia Bernstein's party at their Park Avenue apartment on January 14 1970.

Radical Chic was one of Wolfe's most famous pieces – for the way it showed smart, rich people espousing radical causes a world away from their own lives, but I loved it for other reasons, too. For describing, years before I'd ever been to New York, the A-lister guests, the fashionable decoration of the Bernstein's apartment and what they ate and drank. I wish I'd been there.

I love a night out; I've had quite a lot of nights out, and I miss it when I'm in a sort of semi-purdah because of, say, a book deadline. I've just finished one, and I vowed to be at the club/pub/whatever every night when I was demob happy.

I love seeing how the other halves live. Toffs, profs (scatty, often bad at food and drink but great at inviting clever talkers), shiny celebrities at shiny parties sponsored by shiny businesses. And young people who seem to live on air but make up for it by sheer inventiveness. No vintage anything or Roquefort bits, but great clothes and music.

For decades, I've been able to rationalise any amount of party-going as work. My first real 'day job' was as a market researcher with a brilliant employer who loved mapping trends, so he liked his people to get out there. My first writing job, for the obsessively social and fashion-following *Harpers and Queen* (H&Q) magazine, meant I was honour-bound to go to anything I could. Penniless writers in shiny magazines got a lot of shiny invitations. The important grown-up editors could have gone out several times a night, New York style, seven days a week if they wanted, from the huge kindness of PRs. As a newcomer, I still started on two or so a week, which went up later when I was on the masthead.

The absolute star of *H&Q* then, Mrs Kenward, otherwise 'Jennifer' of Jennifer's Diary, certainly was out practically every night. Back then, she went mainly to parties given by toffs in grand houses, her kind of people. She didn't tell you much about the decoration, food or drink, or any delicious gossip. Her job was to tell you exactly what toffs were there. It seemed as if they were listed in rank order, like a 'Correct Form' table plan. She went on providing this curious service to aspirant readers who wanted their children to marry grandees until she retired in 1991 at the age of 84.

I wish I'd kept a diary. I wish I'd taken pictures – the brilliant Dafydd Jones has been taking smart party pics for *Tatler* and others since the early 1980s. The differently brilliant Richard Young focused on celebrities at those shiny parties. Their photographs bring back a few parties I actually went to and a lot I only wanted to go to.

I can remember the combination of grime and grandeur in some of the upper-class houses I saw in the 1970s before the next generation smarted them up, and sometimes the fascinating stinginess of the food and drink, plus the completely otherworldly things these people said then!

And in my early expeditions among registered clever-dick and big-name writers and academics – usually friends of my clever editor Ann Barr – it turned out they wanted to talk about Hollywood films and celebrity gossip just like everyone else. No intellectual strain for me, then.

I remember with gratitude when I met somebody I'd wanted to meet because our host had made it happen. Putting people together actively is the most brilliant hosting skill. And I can remember times when famous people acted amusingly out of character, as in the famously gnomic Andy Warhol becoming positively voluble in Diane Von Furstenberg's huge New York apartment overlooking the river.

Luke Johnson has been everywhere as a writer, entrepreneur and youthful 1980s Disco Inferno club inventor in Oxford and LA. As an investor, he's specialised in making trillions out of food and hospitality businesses of all kinds, from top-end London restaurants to affordable national chains grown out of small inspirations. He's given a lot of parties, and his parents, as he will tell you, gave and went to every literary/political party in London back in the day. His co-author and colleague Graeme Boyd is from Glasgow, where they know how to have a good time. So, if anyone can tell you how to do it, it's them.

Peter York, April 2024

Introduction

What Are Parties For?

Humans are social animals. We love to gather and celebrate. Eating and drinking are almost invariably involved in such events, as are dancing and entertainment. These festivities have been taking place since time began – an essential part of what makes life worth living. Parties are a vital way societies congregate in friendship when important milestones are remembered, together with an opportunity to forge new relationships.

Some might argue that parties are trivial rituals, social froth of no consequence. I profoundly disagree. Parties often represent the happiest moments of our lives – birthdays, anniversaries, marriages. Laughing, feasting and dancing with loved ones – the very essence of life. So often, defining relationships have been ignited at a party.

In some respects, parties might be considered the summit of human pleasure: they combine friendship, romance, music, food, drink and plenty of jokes. What is more exciting than receiving an unexpected party invitation out of the blue? Limitless possibilities! The anticipation of an evening of glittering company, amusing conversation, delectable food and drink – and the chance to make new friends – what could be better?

Chapter 1

My Party Days

I have loved parties ever since I can remember. My parents were enthusiastic party-givers, regularly hosting lunch and dinner gatherings at our family home for their flamboyant collection of friends, old and new. They were also energetic party-goers, flitting from political soirees to book launches across West London.

It became apparent to me some years ago that certain people take the trouble to host parties, but most others rarely bother. I suppose many form the somewhat selfish position that there is always some other mug foolish enough to assume the financial burden and sheer effort of organising a party and opt to be the perennial guest, never the host.

But they are missing out. Throwing a party can be both a generous act and a source of great pleasure. Of course, it is about showing off, but also about gathering your favourite group of people together in the same place at the same time to commemorate camaraderie – sharing good times with your treasured friends. What could be more pleasurable?

I have so many wonderful memories of throwing parties in all sorts of places – from Brighton Palace Pier to St Thomas' Hospital to The London Library to a nightclub off Hollywood Boulevard. I have enjoyed the entire business – from choosing a location, drawing up the guest list, picking out the songs, deciding on the menu, designing the invitation and then hosting the affair.

I co-hosted parties in Hollywood in the summer of 1982 when my university pal and I launched a club called The English Club. We used the slogan 'New Import Dance Music', and it ran from 9pm to 2am on a Thursday at the Copacabana Club, 1545 North La Brea Avenue, just above Sunset Boulevard. My business partner and I did everything from publicising the evenings by handing out flyers to DJing on the night. I'm not sure our enterprise made money, but it was terrific fun.

Over the decades, I have hosted well over 50 parties, each with 100 guests or more. In doing so, I have been indirectly responsible for kindling many friendships and romances. Some guests subsequently married and had families with people they met at my parties. The power of a party – think of how much happiness you can spread by organising a gathering for your nearest and dearest. What brilliant conversation might flow? What new connections might be forged?

As a guest, I have attended many hundreds of parties – too many to count, from intimate supper parties to vast gatherings of hundreds of people at grand venues like the V&A Museum or banquets at the Guildhall in the City of London. For many years, I have also been the majority owner of a long-established party planner called The Admirable Crichton, run by the indomitable Ruth Lawton-Owen. She has organised hundreds of events for everyone from the royal family to TV celebrities. If you want a brilliant wedding, anniversary, birthday or celebration of any kind, then I recommend the AC! (www.admirable-crichton.co.uk)

Giving a party is also a terrific way to meet new people and make friends. Just ask your guests to bring someone you haven't met. If you are hosting this type of gathering, it's probably best to keep it relatively small so you can spend time and get to know the newcomers. In many ways, parties are the best forum to build new relationships – people are relaxed and in the frame of mind to socialise – they feel safe and welcome.

Throwing a party can be a creative process. You get to choose the guest list, the date, the theme, the venue, the décor, the music, the food and drink, the style of invitation and the entertainment. It is an enjoyable way to thank friends for their companionship. It is also a way to stay in touch with people. Attending a party is a mind-expanding experience – and hosting your own party is the biggest thrill of all.

Accepting a party invitation really means reciprocation at some point in the future. The guest should become the host. If you are invited to dinner by a friend, you feel a social obligation to return the hospitality and ask them for a meal at your home. If you are forever the taker and never the giver, eventually, the invitations disappear. You don't need to give lots of parties – but occasionally, you should try to repay all the kindness you have received from others and invite them in turn.

Sometimes, I take a moment to myself and survey the scene. I'll stand at the back of the room and observe. Every once in a while, there is a synergy where everything clicks into place – the people, the music, the food, the drink. Everyone is happy; everyone is themselves. It's a beautiful feeling and, for the host, makes all the preparation, the organisation, the cost and the hassle of taking care of the small details worthwhile. The other thing about parties is they are slightly addictive! Once you have hosted one, you're bound to throw another in a few months or even sooner. I hope you have as much fun as I do!

Since my teenage years, I have been a compulsive party person, giving and attending gatherings of all sorts. Indeed, parties were a critical element in my choice of career. At Oxford University, I started throwing parties with my friends in our college rooms – mainly to meet girls. However, the college authorities disapproved of such noisy revelry, so my co-hosts and I sought an alternative venue.

We came across a nightclub that was closed on Monday evenings – Scamps in the West Way Centre. Usually, it only catered to local town dwellers and ignored students. We offered to fill it by inviting a student crowd and agreed with the club owners that they would keep the bar takings while we could retain the door money. We called our Monday evenings The Era Club, with the intention that each week, we would concentrate on a particular period of music.

After lots of marketing effort, handing out leaflets and sticking up posters advertising our launch, I arrived half an hour early on the opening night. I was stunned to see a queue of guests had already formed outside. From that moment, it became clear that our party was going to be popular – and it had the potential to become a successful business and a fabulous weekly party.

That initial triumph inspired me to embark on a business career rather than medicine – my undergraduate degree. And so, for over 40 years, I have been active in many aspects of the hospitality, leisure and entertainment industries: nightclubs, restaurants, pubs, hotels, contract catering, brewing, cafes and bakeries, gaming, travel, festivals, theatre, bowling and various other segments. Mainly, it consists of showing guests a great time, serving delicious food and drink, and ensuring they leave full of happy memories – and perhaps a new friend!

Chapter 2

A Brief History of the World's Greatest Parties

The modern-day party guest can lack the sparkle of the partying crowd of 10 or 15 years ago. Nowadays, social media influencers parade through events not because they want to be there but because they are being paid to attend. They are paid to create buzz and awareness for a new service, brand or product and connect this with other influencers. For me, this is as bland a job as they come. I met one recently at the opening of a new restaurant who remained glued to their phone, steadfastly refused any food and drink, offered the barest of small talk and left abruptly without thanking the host. He was likely on his way to the next party to do the same thing all over "again" "poor" soul. I wondered what his passion was. Why bother? I wondered what he thought he would be doing in 20 years when his good looks, stamina and popularity had faded. Little did he know the talent of creative individuals and entrepreneurs within the arts and hospitality sectors who were in attendance. Or, indeed, the convivial and enlightening conversations he could have been having. For me, it was a pleasure to have been invited. And in some ways, it always is. An invitation to another party always adds a spring to my step or can turn a glum day around.

Compare the influencer-infected parties of today to Truman Capote's Black and White Ball in 1966 at the Grand Ballroom of the Plaza Hotel in New York City, aka the most extravagant party of the 20th century! Capote had a vision that once he became rich and famous (following the publication of *In Cold Blood*), he would throw a party for the elite members of high society. Capote drew inspiration from the 'Ascot scene' in *My Fair Lady* in which the women were all dressed in black and white (he described them, quite aptly, as 'swans'). Capote spent $16,000 on the ball – mainly on Taittinger Champagne – quite a bar bill, especially in those days. The party was presented in honour of *Washington Post* editor Katharine Graham, a savvy tactic to increase publicity and focus. The event was described as a "tour de force of social engineering".

Capote laboured extensively for months over the 540-name guest list, whittled down from 1,000. It became much like a book project that Capote dithered over for an entire summer, unable to decide which social, political or cultural 'friend' to invite. Could you imagine the excitement of receiving such an invitation? Back then, it mattered. For years, I have enjoyed glancing at the actual Capote invitation, the eloquent wording and the raised font, the faded colour and the pocket jacket size; just six typed lines with the guest's name handwritten in fountain ink. It offers me similar pleasure to the menus of some of my favourite restaurants I've visited or, indeed, owned. I still think the phrase '...*requests the pleasure of your company*' is one of the most delectable in the English language. Without success, I have tried contacting auction houses worldwide to get my hands on an original invitation, but they are few and far between. Probably one rests within a thrift store book.

Nonetheless, The Museum of the City of New York has an excellent digitised version that is free to access. They also hold a remarkable collection of the dresses worn at the party, with detailed descriptions. Capote's Ball was deemed the pinnacle of New York's social season and has yet to be matched.

Other notable parties include the 'Surrealist Ball' of 1972 at the Château de Ferrières in France. Marie-Hélène de Rothschild and her husband Guy threw a lavish bash for a cast of the most eccentric characters from European high society. The invitations were written backwards, with guests requiring a mirror to read them. The facade of the enormous chateau was lit in red to make it look like it was on fire, and upon entrance, guests had to walk through black ribbons that mimicked cobwebs. Aside from otherworldly costumes and bizarre decorations, guests included Audrey Hepburn and Salvador Dalí. To top it off, servants were dressed as cats!

Literature teems with lavish parties. Some of the best parties I've been to have occurred in bookshops. There's something gratifying about briefly meeting an author who has spent the last three years of their life researching and writing their magnum opus. Even better to buy a signed first edition there and then.

Some of the greatest works of literature have created unforgettable party scenes, be it Bilbo Baggins' 'Eleventy-First' birthday party which opens J. R. R. Tolkien's *Lord of the Rings*, The Mad Hatter's Tea Party from Lewis Carroll's timeless *Alice in Wonderland* or The Netherfield Ball from Jane Austen's *Pride and Prejudice*.

F. Scott Fitzgerald's *The Great Gatsby* captured the tumultuous decade known as the 'Roaring Twenties' when speakeasies flourished as prohibition failed. The three parties in the novel – the Buchanan's gathering, Gatsby's lavish bash and the party at the Plaza Hotel – represent the corruption of the American Dream. I re-read these scenes repeatedly, not for their expressions of grandeur and contentment but because of the vacant selfish aspects of the characters and their inevitable doom. They thought the party would last forever, but it never does. It didn't for Fitzgerald either, a broke and ruined man, dead at 44.

Evelyn Waugh was another novelist from the same era with a great talent for describing fabulous parties. It would be fun to be a character in his two first great books, *Vile Bodies* and *Decline and Fall*. Perhaps the best such get-together is Lady Metroland's in *Vile Bodies* from 1930. The party is in her grand Mayfair house, 'the most beautiful building between Bond Street and Park Lane'. It features the Bright Young People and the American evangelist Mrs Melrose Ape. The latter was surely based on Aimee Semple McPherson, a notorious Los Angeles-based radio preacher. Inevitably, the evening descends into chaos.

Parties have also been integral in bringing famous authors together. In 1928, Sylvia Beach – founder of the Paris-based bookshop Shakespeare and Company – hosted a dinner party for F. Scott Fitzgerald to meet his literary icon, James Joyce. As the story goes, Joyce didn't seem impressed with Fitzgerald's theatrics. It was in 1956, at a party in Cambridge, England, that Sylvia Plath first set eyes on Ted Hughes, igniting a relationship that was ultimately doomed. Maya Angelou was introduced to famed editor Robert Loomis at a dinner party in 1968. Loomis encouraged her to write an autobiography of her upbringing in the segregated South. The classic *I Know Why the Caged Bird Sings* emerged the following year.

Indeed, since time began, I am sure couples have been meeting and falling for each other at parties. In recent years, many relationships have started with dating apps. I am of a generation that didn't have Tinder, Bumble or any online company to meet a romantic partner. And I readily admit to a profound prejudice in favour of the serendipity and drama of meeting someone special at a party rather than the industrial scale choice offered by the internet. How can you assess a personality, a sense of humour, or whether someone has a good heart if it's a split-second glance at a photo and then a swipe left or right?

Regarding gatherings within the world of politics, US President John F. Kennedy's 45th birthday party in 1962 takes some beating. Before a crowd of about 15,000, Marilyn Monroe serenaded the President with a sultry rendition of Happy Birthday To You in the world's most expensive dress.

Another birthday party for the history books was Bianca Jagger's 30th birthday at Studio 54, Manhattan. Bianca paraded around the dance floor on a white horse, led by a nude man covered in gold – as you do! Most people recognise the name Studio 54 and think it went on for decades; such was its popularity. It did, with various owners, but its peak was between 1977 and 1980 when the founders ran it. Those were the golden times. I'd love to have been there. The colourful co-founders – entrepreneurs Steve Rubell and Ian Schrager – not only recognised an opportunity for exclusivity via the infamous guest list but were the first to tap into the burgeoning New York gay scene. Also interesting to note is Uva Harden, a German entrepreneur who had the original idea for Studio 54 but sold out to Rubell and Schrager after funding fell through. Now, where have I heard that before? Rubell and Schrager ended up in jail for tax evasion, and sadly, Steve Rubell died in 1989. Schrager continued in business and is seen as the inventor of the boutique hotel, opening Morgans, Royalton and Paramount in New York, and many others.

The Life and Soul...

I've never much taken to the idea of hellraisers or, even worse, 'party animals'. The media through the ages has shaped such actors, musicians and sports stars with a gloss of empathy or humour, but for me, such behaviour is not only brazen but, at times, endangering. If you delve deeper into the lives of raconteurs like Richard Harris, Peter O'Toole, Peter Finch, Richard Burton and Oliver Reed, you'll realise such hedonism only brought destruction and sadness to otherwise brilliant souls. Most were deeply depressed, with money, personal and legal worries snaring them throughout the peak of their careers and, of course, an over-indulgence in the booze. A great pity.

On the subject of hellraisers, I met Graeme, co-author of this book and a friend of over 20 years, at a party for Condé Nast at their London headquarters. At the time, he wasn't fulfilled working in the basements of Vogue House, so we decided that night that he should come and work for me. We haven't looked back since and have worked on many projects, from books to property to research.

Chapter 3

Invitations You Can't Refuse

"Plan your guest list carefully. That is the key ingredient to any memorable gathering."

Annie Falk

Sitting on the mantelpiece of my London home are various party invitations I've been sent over the past few months. I love receiving invitations and displaying them, especially as there were nearly two lockdown/COVID years when the mantelpiece was bare. I often stare at these invitations and wonder how these parties will go... Will I attend? Will it be worth it? Why did I receive an invitation in the first place? Yet, one thing I always try to consider before accepting is whether I will meet interesting people. A great party can only happen if exciting people are there.

Despite my wife ceremoniously throwing out invitations past their due date, I am often sentimental and keep such invitations from friends from whom I've drifted apart, those who have moved abroad or sadly passed on. Likewise, I tend to keep invitations from businesses I have been a part of or those I helped to grow, for which I'd like to keep a small memento (rather than a 180-page annual report). Such artefacts are worth saving, and I look forward to my children one day looking through them in the same way other families look through photo albums.

I prefer to receive a party invitation in the post rather than an email, text message or phone call. There is something more personal and exciting about opening a posted, sealed envelope.

Writing a party invitation is a fun and creative task. Here's a step-by-step guide to help you write a party invitation:

Start with a warm and inviting greeting:
- "Dear [Name/Group],"
- "You're invited to [Name]'s Party!"

Clearly state the reason for the invitation:
- "Join us to celebrate [occasion/event]!"
- "Come and party with us for [name]'s [birthday/graduation/anniversary]!"

Provide essential details:
- Date: Include the specific date and day of the week.
- Time: Mention the start and end time of the event.
- Venue: Mention the location/address where the party will be held.
- Theme (if applicable): If there's a specific theme for the party, mention it here.
- Dress code (if applicable): If there's a specific dress code, mention it too.

RSVP: Ask the guests to respond by a specific date and provide contact details (email or phone number).

Add a personal touch and build excitement:
- Describe some of the highlights or activities planned for the party.
- Express your enthusiasm and excitement for having them at the event.
- Make the guests feel special and wanted by using phrases like "We would love to have you there" or "Your presence will complete the celebration.
- Adopt a catchy phrase to get the guest's attention:
- 'Wine & Dine'
- 'Cocktails and Conversation'
- 'Boozy & Schmoozy'
- 'Dinner and Dancing'
- 'Booze and Boogie'

Provide additional information:
- Any specific instructions or requests, such as bringing a dish to share or a gift.

- Any surprises or special announcements you want to reveal at the party.

End with a closing note:
- "We can't wait to see you there!"
- "Let's make it a night to remember!"

Sign off:
- "Best regards,"
- "With love,"
- "Yours sincerely,"

Include your name or the host's name and contact information (phone number or email) for further inquiries.

Remember to be clear and concise while including all the necessary details. Feel free to add your own personal flair and style to make the invitation unique and exciting.

Formal and religious events: Weddings, Baptisms/Christenings, Bar and Bat Mitzvahs, First Communions, and Confirmations tend to have set wordings and details.

Go paperless

Digital (eco-friendly) invites have now replaced paper invitations for most people. It's just as easy to contact people digitally as through the post. Guests can also respond with one click! Here are some of my favourites:

Paperless Post has an invite for every occasion. The content team comprises artists, designers, and letterers who create original artwork for online invitations that deliver a sophisticated voice. Paperless Post collaborates with designers and lifestyle brands to create distinctive designs that suit any event.

Evite allows you to select a template from thousands of professionally-designed invites or upload and create your own, then add your event details and send them with a click.

Eventbrite is a central hub for guests to RSVP on a personal event page. Launch a free RSVP website and send paperless invitations with RSVP links to your event website.

Greenvelope works with a community of stationers, illustrators, calligraphers, graphic artists, and painters worldwide to create exclusive, contemporary designs for every style. Its messaging service enables check-ins and updates with guests and removes all the stress of planning.

RSVPify makes organising large-scale events far easier. Easily track RSVPs with a visible traffic-light system showing your invitees' responses.

Punchbowl can be sent via email or text, appearing on your guests' phones within minutes of setting up your event. Pick a design, customise the details and then head to your guests' page to import the contact details of all your invitees. Free!

PurpleTrail lets you browse a gallery of free online invitations and provides paperless invitations with RSVP tracking so you can monitor who is joining you for your event.

Etsy allows you to personally search for unusual and unique invitation templates on the website. Your invite will look unique and different from anything your guests have seen.

As entertaining has become less formal, invitation wording has loosened up. Many party details besides the date, time, place and host are now being shared. Modern etiquette and language keep evolving so much it's hard to keep up with what is good manners and what isn't. Be as clear as you can while writing your invitation to help guests feel relaxed, excited and in the mood to party!

Composing a party invitation can leave you perplexed. Give essential information, but don't go overboard. "There's no doubt that peoples' sensitivities and norms are changing with the times," James Hirschfeld, co-founder and chief executive of Paperless Post told *The Independent*. This online invitation source has more than 175 million users. Only a generation ago, he said, hosts would not have been asking about dietary restrictions or attaching gift registries. "But such are the times we live in." The list of awkward modern entertaining issues continues to grow. "You do have people who just show up for a party with a friend and maybe even bring a dog," Hirschfeld said. "I haven't yet seen 'Your Dog is Not Invited' on an invitation. But it's only a matter of time."

Creative ideas for writing a party invitation

Creative ideas for a party invitation… set the right tone and mood!:

- Boarding Pass: Create an invitation that resembles a boarding pass, complete with details about the party and a "seat number" for the recipient.
- Puzzle Pieces: Print your party details on individual puzzle pieces and send them to your guests. Instruct them to complete the puzzle to view the invitation.
- Message in a Bottle: Roll up your invitation and place it inside a small glass or plastic bottle. Seal the bottle and send it to your guests, evoking a sense of adventure and mystery.
- Comic Book Style: Design your invitation as a comic strip featuring illustrations and speech bubbles to convey all the party details in a fun and visually appealing way.
- VIP Passes: Create personalised VIP passes for each guest, complete with their names and a lanyard. It will make your guests feel special and excited about attending the party.
- Pop-up Cards: Design a card that pops up when opened, revealing the party details creatively and interactively.
- Scratch-off Invitations: Print your party details on cards with a scratch-off surface, like a lottery scratchcard. Scratch off the surface to reveal the party's date, time, and location.
- Movie Ticket Style: Design your invitation to resemble a movie ticket, complete with the party details presented as the "feature presentation," "intermission", etc.
- Treasure Map: Create an invitation that looks like a treasure map, complete with drawn landmarks, clues and instructions leading your guests to the party location.
- Balloon Surprise: Attach a deflated balloon to each invitation with a note instructing guests to blow it up to reveal the party details written on it.

Chapter 4

Taking Care of Business

There was a time when a specific attire was a critical aspect of party-going. Nowadays, dress codes are much less rigid, except for a few events, like The Royal Enclosure at Ascot Races. Specific traditional rules still apply. Black tie means a dinner jacket and bow tie for men and a formal evening dress for women. Business casual means a suit. Fancy dress invitations usually offer a theme – Halloween, for example. Come As You Are is the ultimate informal requirement.

I have rarely stipulated a dress code for any party I've thrown because I want guests to dress in whatever they feel most comfortable wearing – and I hate wearing stuffy garb. That is despite me – somewhat astonishingly – winning the Best Dressed Businessman of the Year Award in 1999, presented by The Menswear Council. I'm sure they confused me with someone else.

Of course, if guests dress up in glamorous clothes, then all the better. My wife puts lots of effort into her party outfits, just as some people adore any opportunity to wear fancy dress. Indeed, for many people, choosing what to wear for a big occasion is a source of joy – and sometimes stress. The more diplomatic and constructive advice you can supply as a host, the better.

Feeling comfortable in what you're wearing is the best way to dress for a party, as long as you honour the event's theme, style and setting. Dress to the occasion and purpose of the party: make sure your outfit feels authentic to you. Also, consider the host because dressing in a way that resonates with the host's taste and fashion sense can show thoughtfulness and a little tact.

Never overdress. Adhere to the dress code and dress appropriately. All my parties are casual, but sometimes I attend formal or black-tie events. The dress code will set the tone for your outfit. Add layers as they add depth to your outfit. Incorporate your style without going overboard. Choose an outfit that complements your shape. Buy a new party outfit that will boost your self-confidence and help you express your unique personality.

If the party has a specific theme, why not incorporate some elements of this into your outfit? Even a small accessory can make all the difference. Subtle accessories can elevate an outfit. Don't be afraid to go for that head-turning look. Why not? It's a party after all. Stand out but in a good way.

Is the party indoors or outdoors? Will it be hosted in a formal venue or somewhere more relaxed? Dress according to the environment. If it's outdoors, you might consider bringing a pocket umbrella. Comfortable shoes are also crucial if you will be standing on your feet for a while.

Darker colours lend a more formal feel, while brighter colours are better for casual occasions.

A well-groomed appearance complements your outfit. Don't forget to take care of personal hygiene. There's nothing worse than talking to someone with bad breath! Smell nice.

Dressing up is a relative term. Remember your style, and don't be afraid to express it. I can't wait to see you!

Any Time is Right for a Party

Many would-be hosts feel they can only throw a party on certain fixed occasions – New Year's Eve, their birthday, wedding, and other well-known dates. This is nonsense. I recommend throwing parties at every (reasonable) opportunity – presuming you have the energy and resources. No excuse is needed!

I advise you to choose occasions when others are not throwing parties and be original. There's no point in everyone hosting a bash on, say, November 5th, December 31st or July 4th – which is what so often happens – so there is enormous duplication. One of the reasons I like throwing a party around my birthday in early February is that it tends to be a fairly bleak time of year, and few others give parties then. Consequently, there is little competition from other party hosts for the most glamorous guests!

There is a fair amount of snobbery regarding protocol at parties. Everything from the invitation to the menu, the music, the venue, the guest list and the place settings. Parties are at the heart of social status and class. Who you invite, where you throw the party, how you organise the evening – these reveal much about you. Never allow all this stuff to put you off hosting an event.

There are also many social conventions with parties – from using French phrases (for example, *RSVP, placement, hor d'oeuvres*) to seating plans and party attire. But, above all, what hosts *should* be is authentic, confident, generous and prepared.

It is natural to follow convention when hosting a party, but I would encourage you to be original – as long as it makes the occasion more pleasurable for your guests. I suppose the protocols have arisen to guide guests and hosts so people don't commit terrible *faux pas*. For example, it is standard practice for dinner party guests to bring a contribution – either a bottle of something sparkling, a box of chocolates, or flowers.

Ultimately, all these social conventions matter much less than who you invite, how you amuse your guests and the mood of the evening. The most unforgettable parties are not the most expensive or poshest affairs, but the occasions where you first met those who became lifelong friends – or perhaps even your future spouse.

Of course, people don't only throw parties for purely social reasons. Many parties are used by charities to raise funds from donors; they serve to launch new businesses or celebrate first nights, reward staff or other stakeholders in an organisation, show corporate clients a good time, for professionals to network, and countless other reasons. Parties punctuate our lives, from childhood birthdays to school prom nights, work functions, weddings, christenings, anniversaries and even wakes.

There are a myriad of parties: from extravagant balls to intimate soirees, from firework-heavy Guy Fawkes nights to refined garden parties – and everything in between. Parties can also occur at any time of day, from breakfast or brunch parties to luncheon parties, afternoon tea parties, early evening cocktail parties, dinner parties and evening dances.

Parties are held to mark the critical passages in life – birth, marriage and death. We arc a gregarious species and feel the need for the company of others when something important happens. These are set pieces. Some parties, like wedding receptions, tend to be somewhat formal – with proper card invitations, speeches and dancing, and all the technical intricacies of a wedding list (suggested gifts for the happy couple). However, many types of parties have no set rules. They can last an hour or all night; be just a few guests or hundreds; offer simple tea and cakes or unlimited alcohol; include loud music, live performances or neither. As host, you get to choose the event you will enjoy, which will inevitably reflect your character – and your budget.

I think carefully about which day of the week I throw a party. Traditionally, Friday and Saturday nights were favourite party evenings because there was no work or school the following day, so guests could stay up later and possibly drink more.

But people often go away at weekends – for a brief trip abroad or to their country residence – so they aren't available for weekend events. Generally, I have tended to host parties on midweek evenings – typically Wednesday or Thursday night. Many people instinctively prefer to avoid going out on a Monday night – it is too early in the work week to let their hair down.

Moreover, only some venues will permit private bookings on Friday or Saturday nights because they are busy. Many bars and clubs shut early in the week and are therefore available for exclusive parties. For the right location, I will hold a party on a Monday evening, because, ultimately, securing the perfect venue is more important than which day you choose.

I never throw parties in August or the second half of July – too many prospective guests are abroad on their summer holiday. The same can apply during half term and Easter holidays. Of course, whichever date you choose, there will be a certain proportion of guests otherwise engaged – but it makes sense to select times of the year when you are likely to maximise attendance.

Timings for parties also matter. I don't bother throwing a party that only lasts an hour or two at most – it is too much effort for too little pleasure. Yet this is the format for many cocktail parties: they start at 6:30pm and end at 8:30pm. Inevitably, most guests don't arrive on the dot and leave well before the end – usually to go out to dinner. So, the average guest stays for no more than an hour.

I like a party to start early and end late so guests feel encouraged to spend the entire evening in each other's company. This means you must keep your guests fed and watered – rather than a fleeting impression, they tend to stay and make a proper night of it.

I have a friend called Jon who lives in a magnificent house in Chelsea, which is ideal for entertaining. He is one of London's greatest and most generous party-givers, and he specialises in what he calls a 'rolling party' – lasting from 5:30pm to 10pm – asking guests to come early or late – whichever suits. He invites many guests, but the event never feels too crowded because there are regular waves of arrivals and departures throughout the evening.

Professional Party Planners

There are many dozens of professional party planners who organise social events for a fee. They tend only to get involved in larger parties – weddings, significant anniversaries and other milestones, corporate bashes and so forth. It is only worth getting such firms on board when you have a decent budget and intend to host a major gathering.

Party planners can sort out a variety of services:

- Finding a venue and negotiating the rental agreement
- Lighting and sound
- Flowers
- Entertainment
- Invitations
- Food and drink
- Catering equipment rental, including tables and chairs
- Security

If you are hosting a significant event, consider using a professional party organiser. Handling all the logistics yourself – especially if you have never done it before – will be difficult, whereas experts know all the most reliable suppliers.

Chapter 5

Venue, Venue, Venue

Deciding on the right location for your party is critical. The setting helps determine if the event will be an outstanding achievement or a damp squib. I can recall hosting parties in all manner of large and small spaces, ranging from a hotel ballroom to town halls to subterranean arches to a library. One of the joys of hosting a party is exploring different venues and using your imagination to see how each setting might work. There are many places keen on generating income from hosting your bash, so you will likely have a lot of options. The decision will be dictated by various factors, including:

- Your budget
- The number of guests you expect to attend
- Venue availability
- Your flexibility about dates and times
- The facilities of the venue and what you plan to provide in terms of refreshment and entertainment

There are many other considerations. Will you need security at the venue? Is it easy to find? Is it in a central location, convenient for your guests? Is there parking and is it close to public transport connections? Are there sufficient toilet facilities? What about disabled access? How do they organise the cloakroom? Does the venue supply food and drink, or can you handle the catering yourself? What is the kitchen like? Who will do the clearing up? If you are putting on entertainment – for example, live music or a DJ – does the venue have a PA/sound system?

You need to consider carefully the atmosphere of the venue. I recall hosting a party at St John's Hyde Park, near Paddington in London. It is a splendid Gothic revival church with a capacity for a congregation of 700.

As our guests arrived, they were astounded at the spectacular interior of this working church. The grand surroundings and superb acoustics added enormously to the evening and helped make it an excellent birthday party. In addition, Hugh Cornwell of The Stranglers played a marvellous solo set of his greatest hits.

Another brilliant location for one of my birthday parties was the roof of the citizenM hotel opposite the Tower of London. On the 7th floor, the view is spectacular, encompassing the River Thames, Tower Bridge and much of the City of London. Luckily, my business partner Chris Mitchell of Genuine Dining was managing the food offer for CitizenM, so we were given VIP treatment.

The high-level choice of venues boils down to the following:

- Home
- Bar/nightclub/pub function room
- Hotel
- Municipal hall

Take your time to choose the right location, and be fussy. Don't settle for the first space you see. Imagine what it would be like full of bubbly guests one evening. What are the acoustics like? Is there a place for people to dance? Is it an obvious choice? I love finding new spaces. For over a decade, I have organised an annual event in London for alumni of my Oxford college, and one of the great pleasures is identifying a new location each year to delight the guests. From a basement club for military veterans to a Thames boathouse, we have secured all manner of quirky venues. It isn't easy, because we need a space catering to 500 guests.

Of course, many hosts prefer their own homes – for reasons of cost or intimacy. Except for dinner parties, I tend to avoid using my house. I prefer not to have to do the clearing up and relish surprising guests with new locations. Also, some people are nervous that their carpets will suffer from red wine stains or the like. However, external venues require more preparation and expense to ensure the space delivers the right experience.

Every Christmas, a famous friend used to host a splendid bash in his magnificent house overlooking Fitzroy Square in London. The houses on two sides of the square were designed by renowned architect Robert Adam, and our friend felt that such a marvellous home should be thrown open to many guests once a year. The party usually featured a musical interlude, when a pianist, singer or quartet would perform a classical recital.

If the weather is good enough, throwing an outdoor bash in your garden or the local park is always possible. However, unless you rent a marquee, then outdoor functions are always subject to the weather and, as the British know well, it can never be relied upon in our rainy islands. Consequently, I tend to prefer indoor events. There are already enough variables to staging any party – adding the threat of a washout has always put me off staging al fresco occasions.

In cities like London, there are thousands of places for hire all across the capital. Many pubs have basement cellars or first floors that rent privately; hotels typically have several function rooms; nightclubs and bars are often available for exclusive use on nights they would otherwise be shut. Museums, galleries, members' club premises, churches, cinemas, theatres, bowling alleys, studios and various other buildings can also be let for parties.

There are various specialist agencies and websites which market venues for hire. Simple online searches will yield plenty of results for major cities and towns. I like to approach venues directly, but operators like www.designmynight.com, www.tagvenue.com, and www.hirespace.com offer dozens of choices in London. It all depends on budget, number of guests, preferred location, date, party style, etc. Mostly, such intermediaries charge the venue rather than the party host.

You need to think carefully about whether your preferred venues are appropriate for the season: a marquee in a garden can be brilliant in the summer, but at Christmas, you will need a different type of structure. No one likes going to a party that is either suffocatingly hot or freezing cold. All great hosts plan ahead to ensure their guests have an enjoyable time and are comfortable.

One of the reasons you should pick the right location is your turnout will be greater. When I owned the original Ivy restaurant in Covent Garden, I knew that attendance for a party in the first-floor function room was always high. Superb food, drinks and service were guaranteed, all delivered in one of London's most glamorous and famous rooms.

The price to rent a venue varies enormously, depending on location, size, date and what you plan to do about food, drink and entertainment. Plenty of function rooms are available on the basis that if guests turn up and buy drinks and/or food, then there is no rental charge. You can either stick cash behind the bar or tell guests it's a cash bar because you're on a tight budget. In such circumstances, I think you should provide some snacks to eat, as a minimum.

Practical issues are essential when it comes to party venues. Will a loud bash disturb the neighbours? If so, warn them in advance and preferably invite them! Will your guests be able to find the location? Ensure your invitation includes accurate and adequate directions to the venue. Is the venue accessible by various forms of transport? If people have to drive, how will they get home if they have been drinking alcohol? Public transport options like buses and trains are plentiful in cities like London and continue until relatively late. And there are more expensive options like taxis. But if you choose to host a party in a more remote location, consider how guests will get home – otherwise, they may decide not to attend or stay far too sober, worrying about their homeward journey!

While spur-of-the-moment gatherings are fun, most parties need plenty of planning in advance – partly because desirable venues get booked up. Moreover, like many things in life – holidays, for example – anticipating the grand celebration is much of the pleasure. Hence, it would be best to organise the occasion properly to ensure everything goes well.

Chapter 6

The Host With The Most

"Giving a party is very like having a baby; its conception is more fun than its completion, and once you have begun it, it is almost impossible to stop."

Jan Struther

In a way, parties are a branch of show business. You are offering entertainment for your friends – not for profit, of course, but to provide enjoyment. A host is an impresario of sorts.

Successful parties bear the signature of the host – your taste in décor, venue, food, drink, invitation, music and entertainment. Never allow a party organiser to dictate these things: by all means, accept suggestions, but make sure you like them! Your party should reflect your personality and life, from the guest list to the surroundings.

The host of a party is the Master (or Mistress) of Ceremonies and should be directing events to ensure the occasion proceeds as planned. If you employ a party planner, they may well take charge of aspects like the food and drink, but as host, you should be on duty at all times to ensure attendees are happy. This means you need to move around the event, making your guests feel at ease, greeting and introducing them to each other, ensuring they have enough to eat and drink, and helping to create the right atmosphere.

I generally only have one drink at my events because I want to remain *almost* sober in case of emergencies and to take care of my guests. I host parties with my wife, and she and I divide and conquer: one of the reasons to co-host parties is that you can mingle and talk to many more guests than if you are managing proceedings solo.

Of course, if you are the host, guests will come up to you to say hello or goodbye all evening. This means you can rarely have elaborate conversations with your friends if it's a big event. You need to be democratic and spread your attention among the guests. You must never hide away in a corner or the kitchen – you have to be out front, helping the occasion go with a bang, monitoring proceedings to ensure everyone is looked after.

Being a host involves a degree of showmanship. You need to be in good spirits to help lift those of your guests. The perfect host remembers absolutely everyone's name, makes all the guests feel at ease, makes jokes and ensures guests always have enough to eat and drink. A great host is on the move, introducing strangers and making sure the music is at the right tempo and the ambience in the room is welcoming. Of course, none of us are perfect hosts – but great guests are forgiving and appreciate being invited!

An experienced host regularly scans the room to check that guests are mingling and no one is left out. Don't let the room break into insular cliques – ensure your old pals aren't just talking to each other but are also making new acquaintances. Shy newcomers will need some help, so organise introductions. At small events, it is pretty easy to remember everyone's name – at larger parties, this can be difficult and lead to embarrassment. Put effort in before the event by studying the guest list.

Some hosts enjoy giving speeches at their parties. I seldom deliver a speech as it interrupts the flow of conviviality. Such set pieces are only necessary if the occasion is a particular sort of party, such as a book launch or a wedding, with a special message to transmit or etiquette to follow. Occasional announcements can be necessary – "Don't forget to try the birthday cake!" and so forth, but make them very short and to the point.

If you need to make a speech, keep it concise. Never give a rambling, self-indulgent address. My father, who was an outstanding orator, gave me a good piece of advice about speeches. He told me to always make a speech briefer than the audience is expecting.

Only attempt a speech if you are relaxed about public speaking. If you do decide to speak, note the key points you want to convey beforehand. Don't attempt humour unless you have a skill for telling jokes. If there is to be a speech – or God forbid more than one – do it early in the evening, when the crowd is likely to be relatively sober and more receptive to such interventions.

I recall attending a party to celebrate the launch of a ship in Norway. At the end of the dinner, one attendee after another stood up to give a speech.

Most of the impromptu orators were pretty drunk. After about ten of these speeches – all in Norwegian, of course – I made my excuses and left. Clearly, in some countries, it is the custom for almost everyone to give a speech on such occasions. Thank God we don't all embrace that habit!

In her book *The Art of the Visit*, Kathy Bertone lists several attributes every host should possess. She says a host should be:

- Welcoming
- A Master Planner
- Gracious
- A Picture of Restraint
- In the Moment
- A Great Communicator
- A Skilled Ringleader
- Flexible
- Cool Under Pressure
- A Diplomat

That's quite the list – but if you do manage to embody all these qualities, you can be sure your parties will be a hit.

Chapter 7

Be My Guest

"There were some intellectual sharks, some arrivistes, some sheep, good souls, professors, editors, some radicals, who themselves invite poets, novelists, sophomore rioters, and visiting Englishmen..."

Renata Adler

Of course, the guest list is *the* single most important ingredient of any party. The attendees will make or break the event. Select the right mix of engaging and compatible people, and they will have a good time. But if there is no chemistry between the guests – as can happen at certain weddings, for example, where often very disparate guests attempt to mingle – then the party can end in a flop, or even fighting can break out between families and generations!

I have been to too many parties over the years where the surroundings were glittering, the food and drink delicious, but the other guests seemed as dull as dishwater. Many corporate functions are like this – swarming with men in suits, hustling for new clients. Inevitably, I tend to leave such events pretty quickly. By contrast, I've been to parties with basic refreshments held in uninspiring buildings – but the company was scintillating. Of course, those are the parties you remember.

The most fabulous parties have guests who will turn up and fill the room with sparkling conversation and laughter. Invite people who will radiate energy. The most important contribution your guests should make is that they need to be in the mood to enjoy themselves. You want extroverted guests (at least on the night) who enjoy meeting new people and, ideally, have something original to say. Of course, not everyone is going to be fascinating – but you need enough charisma in the place to light a social fire.

You should decide on a few fundamental principles: How many guests will attend? Will you try to balance out the sexes? Will you only invite close acquaintances? Do you have everyone's contact details? Will the party be multi-generational? Will you invite your extended family or just friends?

Remember, not everyone who accepts an invitation will attend on the night. I assume a roughly 20 per cent dropout rate for a larger affair. There are so many reasons why guests cannot turn up – illness, work, family crisis, sudden attacks of shyness or laziness. In any event, don't expect total attendance, and don't be too upset if friends cannot make it. There will be other parties!

If you have a more intimate affair, then you may have to exclude some names. Some friends may feel hurt if they discover they have been left out. It's one reason I like throwing pretty large parties and inviting more or less everyone I consider a friend. Of course, with 100-plus guests, time spent talking to all your pals will be limited. But you spread a lot of pleasure, and people find ways to amuse themselves readily enough.

If you host a bigger party, you can afford to take risks with your guest list. Invite recent acquaintances and those with whom you've almost lost touch. Extend invitations to a good mixture of people – from different backgrounds, professions and with a variety of personalities. Too often, hosts only seem to know those in the same line of work or from a similar part of the world. A great party should deliver surprises – and meeting a diverse selection of people and some familiar faces can be an essential part of that experience.

Who do you invite if you don't have a wide circle of friends? You could ask work colleagues, neighbours, members of your health club or other organisations you frequent. Many people I know seem to make friends with other parents whose children are friends with their children. Use Facebook, LinkedIn or other social networks to connect with people with common interests.

During lockdown, my wife and I celebrated our 'wedding' again (only such formal events were permitted) with a few close friends and invited several acquaintances from Twitter. Many of us had never met in person, and it was the first real-life party almost all of us had attended for over a year. Naturally, it was a huge success. The fact it was a somewhat illicit gathering made it all the more exhilarating. No wonder Speakeasies during Prohibition in the Roaring Twenties were so popular!

One tricky issue is the subject of partners: should you automatically invite other halves? Mostly, it is assumed that spouses and boy/girlfriends are welcome – unless it is a seated affair, in which case, as a guest, you should clarify in advance if they are expected. As host, you must make it clear either way. The one advantage of people coming on their own is they are obliged to mingle, which means they will meet new friends. And that is the dynamite that elevates a so-so party into the stratosphere – making the acquaintance of groovy new people.

Things have changed since Maud C. Cooke wrote in her 1896 book *Social Etiquette: or Manners and Customs of Polite Society*, "There are certain rules to be observed in the writing of invitations which cannot be transgressed." Who you invite to your party and how you do it is up to you – as long as you think everyone will get on.

Ensure you tell guests if they should or shouldn't bring gifts, if it's a birthday or an anniversary. Expect dinner party guests to bring a bottle, a box of chocolates or flowers. You can sometimes agree with close friends that they bring a homemade dessert.

I think at every party I've hosted, I've had at least one co-host. These days, it is invariably my lovely wife, Liza. At university and in my twenties, it was alongside close friends like Hugh, Sudip and Niall. I strongly recommend finding a partner when you throw a party. It spreads the work and cost and means you have two sets of friends mingling.

You should divide responsibilities: one can take care of booking the venue; one can handle the food and drink; one can organise music and entertainment; one can sort out invitations. Of course, you should both draw up the guest list – the combination of two address books will give the evening an added frisson of excitement.

Chapter 8

The Art of Party Conversation

"The only thing that guarantees an open-ended collaboration among human beings, the only thing that guarantees that this project is truly open-ended, is a willingness to have our beliefs and behaviours modified by the power of conversation."

Sam Harris

Conversation is a two-way street. Simply put, the key to a great conversation at a party is being a good listener and showing a genuine interest in what others say. Active listening is easier said than done, but it's a skill we can continually improve. You listen to someone with all your senses, from their body language to the tone of their voice. What is it the person is trying to say? What is their point?

As a host, I've always tried to be engaged and learn something new, ideally from someone new. Most people listen only to respond. They are not attentive listeners; they are only waiting for the moment to speak, jump in and prove themselves right. When they talk, they are in control. They don't have to hear anything they're not interested in. Remember, a good conversation isn't a contest.

I would hate to think of the amount of board meetings and AGMs I have sat through and observed this, even from seasoned veterans. Don't enter a competition with your other guests. Nobody is there to win, even if it is at the expense of your ego. When the person you are speaking to is offering you their full attention, then you know it: you can tell from their eyes.

We all lead interesting lives and have important careers, even if we don't think we do. You will undoubtedly have a diverse group of friends: some rich and successful, some not so wealthy but equally successful, some going through a crisis or a problem of some sort, some sailing smoothly on, or some with different political perspectives than you. No matter – a diverse group of people is always the best bunch at a party! Who would want to go to a party with a group of affable doppelgangers? Boring.

Below are some tips to keep the conversation flowing smoothly at a party.

Introduce yourself (if required). Start with small talk, build a rapport, and then go further! Have the courage to move beyond small talk. Start a conversation that matters. Go on a journey with the other guests. Contemplate someone else's ideas. Personal questions are good as they break the ice and allow the other person to speak about something familiar. Don't complain or moan – instead, offer solutions. Don't judge – instead, offer empathy. Don't dominate the conversation, don't brag, or get stuck on one topic. Go easy on cracking jokes or trying to be overly funny when you first meet someone. It usually fails. Remember, you are not a storyteller or an all-knowing soothsayer. You can share the air, but if it's all about you – all surface-level – you're doing something wrong.

"The great charm of conversation consists less in the display of one's own wit and intelligence than in the power to draw forth the resources of others"

Jean de la Bruyère

Ask open-ended and meaningful questions. Questions elicit answers. Try to dig deeper than the superficial. Don't just nod and say yes or no, pretending to be inquisitive. Engage in critical thought. Think before you speak; use words clearly and accurately. Have some relatable examples and share your own viewpoints and personal experiences. Expressing your opinion is fine, but don't force it on your guests. Try hard to avoid criticising, judging or being spiteful. Converse – don't debate or argue. Remember, asking personal questions signals your interest in that person. Make them feel good about themselves! They are there to have fun.

"The real art of conversation is not only to say the right thing at the right place but to leave unsaid the wrong thing at the tempting moment."

Lady Dorothy Nevill

Admit what you don't know. There is nothing wrong with showing you don't understand something – this can even be flattering. Even better, ask them to explain their point again – perhaps in a different way.

"All conversation is a magnetic experiment."

Ralph Waldo Emerson

Embrace silence. There is nothing awkward about silence. A few moments of silence are a way to reflect, think and transition. Collect yourself, take in the room, and take a measured breath. Appreciate not speaking. Keeping your mouth shut can often work wonders! Don't fill space with meaningless words. People sometimes don't ask questions because it's not culturally appropriate or because they think it may be invasive. Or maybe they are shy or overly sensitive. I'm quite a shy person at heart, but it doesn't stop me from hosting many great parties!

Find common ground. Find context. Context forms the basis of conversation. A little context from your guest will enable you to form a steady and genuine basis of discussion. Without it, you may well fall flat. Stay curious: everyone has something to teach and something to say. There will always be commonalities between people – embrace such differences. Find and work on common links – the effort will be rewarded.

A useful method great conversationalists use is taking notes. I would be lost without my notebook, which I take with me everywhere. I often write things down immediately, as I'm more likely to remember them. Some of the most significant business ideas I've ever had have been written in my notebook or on the back of a beer mat or napkin.

Remember, not everybody has an encyclopaedic mind – or a first-class degree. Be at one with different types of intelligence among your guests: some will have more than one (known as 'multiple intelligences'). I have a good friend who is a leading cancer practitioner, but I also have one who is a barista in my favourite cafe. I enjoy their company equally and learn from each in a completely different manner. Intelligence is varied and subjective. What's important is learning from such different types as emotional intelligence, body intelligence, linguistic intelligence, naturalistic intelligence… the list goes on, to just being street smart. At a great party, a zoo of human conditions and new knowledge awaits you! Tap right in!

Navigating the minefield of conversation at parties is about a series of steps. Try early on to discover some common ground.

I occasionally give speeches to businesses, charities, academic institutions and entrepreneurial conferences. After the speech, I enjoy speaking to the guests who have sat through my speech and stayed to ask me individual questions. Often, they have passions about a business I've been involved with, or they might have an idea for me to look over. Often, if somebody has come to hear me speak, it's likely they will know a little bit about me and have a genuine interest in wanting to talk to me. It's the same for parties.

Plenty of people come because they haven't seen me or my family in a while or they've just not found the time, something of which I am also guilty. That's the key. Throwing a party because we are all so damned busy in this thing called life – the feeling that if I don't, it's unlikely we'll see each other again for many months – even years. I've certainly never had the attitude that I will wait for someone else to do it.

I commonly give out my business card for my work or personal email to people whose company I have enjoyed. I like email – always have – because it offers me a reference: emails are quick, cost-effective and professional. I can save the person as a contact and easily find them again if something arises in the future that I think might be of interest to them.

The writer, Kovie Biakolo believes: "One of the most important aspects of being a great conversationalist is reading. Reading current events, reading fun things, reading dense things, reading things that expand your views on certain subjects, reading things you like and agree with and reading things you don't agree with. The latter is most important because that is fundamental to understanding different perspectives of the world. You learn nothing new from reading things you already know about or agree with. But all reading increases knowledge and improves vocabulary."

"The air is alive with chatter and laughter, and casual innuendo and introductions forgotten on the spot and enthusiastic meetings between who never knew each other's names."

F Scott Fitzgerald

Good conversationalists are articulate with their word choice, active listeners and critical thinkers who want to learn from their conversational partner. I'm always amazed at what I can absorb from others just from a few minutes of conversation. Adopt a generous spirit that will allow you to be genuinely interested in other people and what they have to say... and the conversation will flow swimmingly.

"There is no such thing as a worthless conversation, provided you know what to listen for. And questions are the breath of life for a conversation."

James Nathan Miller

Chapter 9

Music To My Ears

"The man that hath no music in himself,
Nor is not moved with concord of sweet sounds,
Is for treasons, stratagems, and spoils;
The Motions of his spirit are dull as night,
And his affections dark as Erebus.
Let no such man be trusted. Mark Music."

William Shakespeare

Parties tend to divide into events with accompanying music and those without – events that are all about the conversation. Music can either be in the background or a central element. At most parties where the music is a major part of the festivities, dancing will be involved.

Dancing is an ancient human ritual and can be a joyous activity – even for those no longer in the first flush of youth. I have been to a great 60th birthday party where the guests were strutting their stuff on the floor to an Abba tribute act in a huge marquee. It was quite a scene.

Lively conversation is the true heart of any party, so music should generally not be so loud that it drowns out talk. If your space is large enough, you can increase the volume near the dance floor, or perhaps you can decide to have music only in certain rooms.

DJ culture stands at a juncture of performance, culture and technology. I'm amazed that so many nightclubs have reopened and returned to business after COVID-19, but this shows the resilience and timelessness of the industry. I've respected the history and culture of DJing and record collecting since my student days at Oxford University. Running nightclubs ignited the entrepreneurial fire within me. Indeed, great music at a party is essential for a lively and fun atmosphere.

Confident DJs possess a combination of technical skills (beatmatching, mashups and mixing), musical knowledge (track selection and musical progression) and showmanship (body language and stage presence). Aside from technical proficiency and musical knowledge, they can also read and entertain the crowd. They will be passionate, dedicated and meticulously prepared. Ultimately, a great DJ can connect with your guests, create memorable experiences and leave a lasting impression through their music and performance.

For larger parties, I tend to hire a DJ from a local nightclub who can bring their own PA system, turntables and vinyl (prices vary widely depending on the DJ's experience and equipment). Ask for recommendations from friends, family, and local nightclubs and research social media platforms, websites and review sites. Hiring a DJ involves careful planning and communication to ensure they understand your expectations, can curate sets to suit the occasion and can deliver the desired musical experience for your event.

Clarify cancellation policies and contingency plans in case the DJ cancels at the last minute, which has happened to me on more than one occasion. A basic contract outlining the terms of the agreement, including the date, time, payment details, and any special requests, is worth preparing for both parties. You need to know the DJ's reputation, style, availability and track record. I find hiring DJs to be excellent value for money for the service they provide. To create a memorable and enjoyable party, it's best to have a simple pre-dialogue with the DJ so they can get a feel for who you are, the theme of your party and the vibe of the guests. Remember that parties can present an eclectic mix of attendees with varying tastes and trends.

The chosen songs or playlist must seamlessly blend with the occasion. I prefer playing music from new bands and artists rather than established classics. I enjoy browsing at popular and established record shops in London such as Honest Jon's, Rough Trade and Third Man to see what's new and recommended. DJs can change the whole atmosphere, mood and energy level of a party with one track, so they occupy quite a responsible position, adding more spice to the party.

These days, it's easy to create a designated song request list where guests can suggest songs. You can use a QR code for this, located near the DJ booth and easy for guests to see and scan into their phones. The DJ is also in charge of the music, lighting, visuals and any technical issues (they need to be aware of power outlets or space restrictions). They should have a backup music source if something goes wrong with the primary setup. Ideally, they should be at the venue an hour before the party starts to set up. Ultimately, they need to be adaptable. They can adjust the playlist, skip songs, and control the volume to a level that suits the party atmosphere but doesn't disturb the neighbours.

The best DJs tend to start with more mellow tunes and gradually increase the energy levels as the night goes on while mixing up different genres and tempos to keep things exciting and fun! They know when to build up excitement or when to bring it down. As the party winds down, they gradually transition to quieter and more soothing music to signal to your guests that it's time to leave. The best dance floors are well-lit, inviting and have enough room for dancing. As a host, you must have a little boogie – that goes without saying.

DJs tend to crank the volume up, so you brief them in advance to explain that your guests must be able to converse without shouting. The same applies to live performances unless it is a short set. We have all been to clubs or parties where the music was so loud that communication was impossible. This is a great mistake, and your party will be all the poorer for it if the amplification is too enthusiastic.

If there is no live performance, the music can be provided by a DJ or recorded in advance and played through the sound system. I am somewhat biased: I prefer an actual DJ since I used to spin the discs about 40 years ago – I still have hundreds of vinyl 45 rpm records! A skilled DJ can adjust song sequences to match room tempo, something planned ordering can't do. However, I'm not keen on party DJs who want to give a running commentary – they should be there strictly for the music.

It is essential to calibrate the music thoughtfully according to the age and background of the guests. It is surprising how often you can hear hardcore dance music at a party dominated by sixty-something guests – because they hired the wrong DJ. If you have obscure musical tastes, I suggest you ask someone with more mainstream listening habits to plan the artists and songs to be played.

If you want people to dance, you need familiar floor fillers. I will not bother to recite the tracks, but we all know the classic dance tunes when we hear them. Many are decades old, but that doesn't matter; what matters is that guests enjoy them and are willing to get up on the dance floor as soon as they hear the opening bars.

Organising live acts for a party can be tricky. There are thousands of jobbing musicians – both solo artists and bands – who are available for hire. But only good ones are sufficiently professional to deliver. Unless the performers are of a minimum standard, then I wouldn't bother. And that means you must be prepared to pay a fair sum for the entertainment – unless you have friends who will do it for a discount or for free – and are suitably talented!

You will need a band or solo performer with a broad enough appeal for all the guests to enjoy the show. Resist the temptation to book an act whose tunes and style are so obscure they only attract a tiny minority in the room. And make sure you agree on the length of the set in advance – I would say an hour at most is sufficient for most events, although perhaps two short sets is the best combination.

You will also need to choose the style of music you think suits your bash: Jazz? Swing? Acoustic? Rock'n'roll? Disco? Soul? Classical? The variety of musicians available for hire is remarkable, especially if you have a budget of over £1,000. Ideally, you should see them perform first in person before making a booking to demonstrate that they know how to work a room and that their repertoire is to your liking. If that is impossible, most of the best performers have an online presence that will show them in action.

Other Entertainment

Music is not the only form of amusement you can have at parties. I have hired wandering magicians who mingle among your guests and surprise them with close-up card tricks. If you pick the right performer, they can be a memorable addition to the evening. Similarly, caricaturists can sketch your guests on request, so they take home a souvenir! In the same vein, a mobile photo booth allows your guests to take a set of boisterous snaps to remind them of your party.

Many people love having their fortune told by a tarot card reader: such experts can be hired for a few hours to add a touch of mystery to the evening. Specialist agencies tout every form of entertainment: fire eaters, jugglers, mind readers, singing waiters – there are many 'resting' performance artists who work part-time delighting party guests.

None of these features are cheap, but they do add to the life and soul of the party. As ever, it is essential to ensure such entertainers will fit in with the atmosphere of the room and that you highlight their presence to your guests. People are often shy, so they might need a little coaxing to have their fortune read or a cartoon portrait drawn.

Chapter 10

Food and Drink

"Then I commend mirth, because a man hath no better thing under the sun, than to eat, and to drink, and to be merry: for that shall abide with him of his labour the days of his life, which God giveth him under the sun."

Ecclesiastes 8:15

Food is an essential element of most parties – indeed, the vast majority of get-togethers are based around either the midday or evening meal – and occasionally even breakfast. People have been symbolically breaking bread together as a form of friendship since time immemorial. Eating a shared meal with companions is a central aspect of being human. So when you throw a party, it is crucial to get the food right.

You can only decide what food to serve – and how much – when you have determined the venue and how many guests you plan to invite. If you lack culinary skills and can afford it, I strongly recommend hiring a decent caterer to prepare and serve the food. It means you are free to enjoy the event. Very early on, you will need to choose between providing a more formal sit-down meal, a buffet or canapes. This depends on your budget and location.

I prefer buffets or canapes because they allow guests to mingle. Sit-down meals tie guests to a fixed seat and table, which inhibits the chance interactions that mark a truly successful party. The entire process of having armies of staff come and serve guests identical plates of food while seated seems outdated. I prefer arrangements where guests can help themselves, choosing from various dishes in an appetising display.

Of course, you can stage a sit-down dinner and then encourage mingling, dancing and so forth after the meal. In these situations, I suggest a menu swiftly served and consumed so guests have plenty of time to chat with various people.

Classic buffet dishes, like salads, sandwiches, quiches, cured meats and poached salmon taste good at room temperature. My buffet favourites include sausage rolls, cheese straws, spring rolls, empanadas, ham croquetas, crudites, and Spanish tortilla. Avoid messy foods or those that don't hold well when sitting for a while (like souffles), and pick dishes that can be divided into suitable portions. Almost all these foods can be prepared in advance, so there is no need for cooking on-site, which means you can use venues with no kitchen.

The appearance of food on a buffet display matters enormously. We partly eat with our eyes, and a delicious-looking display of edibles will be consumed much more readily than an unappetising arrangement. The right blend of dishes and the correct crockery are part of the secret.

Organise the buffet table intelligently to ease the flow of guests and speed up service. At all too many parties, a large queue develops of guests waiting to get their meal because of bottlenecks. Ideally, you should set up two sets of identical dishes in a logical order to serve twice as many people.

The sequence of items on the buffet table matters. Plates are at the start, followed by salads, main courses, bread, sauces, butter, napkins and cutlery. Ensure everything is within easy reach and that the correct serving utensils are available. Do use cards for each dish to tell guests what it is if it isn't obvious and in case of allergies. As always, ensure a selection of vegetarian and vegan options.

I never understand why a waiter or waitress passes by with a tray of nibbles without explaining what they are. Presentation can make a big difference, so garnish your canapés with fresh herbs, microgreens, or other decorative touches to make them visually appealing. Everything should be clearly labelled and described for allergens.

Guests want to know what they are eating. Remember to consider any dietary restrictions or preferences your guests may have when planning your nibbles so that everyone can enjoy them. The key is to have a variety of options to cater to different tastes and dietary needs while keeping things bite-sized and easy to handle at your party. Much like music, nibbles can vary widely depending on the theme and style of the party.

Do serve enough food so guests do not go hungry. However, I don't think you need to offer such a lavish spread as Samuel Pepys, the famous diarist, did for his annual lunch to celebrate having a kidney stone removed:

"…I had a pretty dinner for them – viz: a brace of stewed Carps, six roasted chicken, and a Jowle of salmon hot, for the first course – a Tanzy and two neats' tongues and cheese the second. And were very merry all the afternoon, talking and singing and piping on the Flagelette." And this was for six guests!

Some of the best party food is often the most simple. Essentially, guests want just a mouthful or two. Hopefully, they will be too busy talking and drinking to eat!

Here are some of my favourites, with some simple recipes:

Charcuterie Board

Creating a charcuterie board with various cheeses, cured meats, crackers and some fresh fruits or nuts is a wonderful way to impress your guests with a variety of flavours and textures.

Ingredients:

Cheeses:
1. Brie: Creamy and mild.
2. Cheddar: Sharp and firm.
3. Gouda: Nutty and semi-hard.
4. Blue Cheese: Tangy and crumbly.
5. Goat Cheese: Creamy and tangy.

Cured Meats:
1. Prosciutto: Thinly sliced and salty.
2. Salami: Choose a variety, such as Genoa or Soppressata.
3. Chorizo: Spicy and flavourful.
4. Coppa: Dry-cured pork shoulder, thinly sliced.

Crackers and Bread:
1. Baguette Slices: Lightly toasted.
2. Water Crackers: Neutral, allowing the flavours to shine.
3. Grilled Bread: Brushed with olive oil for a rustic touch.

Fresh Fruits:
1. Grapes: Red and green for sweetness.
2. Figs: Fresh or dried, adding sweetness and texture.
3. Apple Slices: Crisp and refreshing.
4. Berries: Strawberries or raspberries for colour and freshness.

Nuts:
1. Almonds: Marcona almonds add a unique touch.
2. Walnuts: Pairs well with cheese.
3. Pecans: Sweet and buttery.

Additional Condiments:
1. Honey: Drizzle over blue cheese or goat cheese.
2. Fig or Fruit Jam: Perfect for pairing with Brie.
3. Mustard: Whole grain or Dijon for meats.
4. Olives: Green and black varieties.

Instructions:
1. Preparation:
   - Arrange cheeses on the board, leaving space between each variety
   - Fold or roll cured meats and place them around the cheeses.
   - Fill in the gaps with fresh fruits, nuts and olives.

2. Bread and Crackers:
   - Arrange a mix of toasted baguette slices, water crackers and grilled bread.
   - Place them in different areas of the board for easy access.

3. Garnishes:
   - Sprinkle fresh herbs like rosemary or thyme over the board for aroma.
   - Add edible flowers for a decorative touch.

4. Condiments:
   - Place small bowls or jars of honey, fig jam and mustard strategically on the board.
   - Ensure guests can easily reach for these accompaniments.

5. Aesthetics:
   - Create a balanced look with a variety of colours and shapes.
   - Consider the visual appeal by arranging items in clusters.

6. Serve:
   - Set out small cheese knives and utensils for spreading condiments.
   - Encourage guests to mix and match flavours.

The key is to offer a diverse selection and let your guests enjoy the experience of combining different flavours. Adjust quantities based on the number of guests and feel free to customise the board based on personal preferences and dietary restrictions. Enjoy your charcuterie board party!

Cheese Straws

Cheese straws are a delightful and easy-to-make appetiser that's perfect for parties. Here's a simple recipe for you to try:

Ingredients:
- 1 1/2 cups grated cheddar cheese
- 1/2 cup unsalted butter, softened
- 1 3/4 cups all-purpose flour
- 1/2 teaspoon salt
- 1/4 teaspoon cayenne pepper (adjust to taste)
- 1/4 teaspoon smoked paprika
- 1/4 cup cold water
- Optional: Sesame or poppy seeds for coating

Instructions:
1. Preheat your oven to 350°F (175°C).
2. Prepare the dough: In a large mixing bowl, combine the grated cheddar cheese and softened butter. Mix until well combined.
3. Add dry ingredients: In a separate bowl, whisk together the flour, salt, cayenne pepper and smoked paprika. Gradually add this dry mixture to the cheese and butter mixture, stirring continuously.
4. Form the dough: Add cold water to the dough, one tablespoon at a time, until the mixture forms a dough. It should be pliable but not too sticky.
5. Roll out the dough: On a lightly floured surface, roll out the dough into a rectangle with a thickness of about 1/4 inch.
6. Cut into strips: Use a sharp knife or a pizza cutter to cut the dough into thin strips, about 1/2 inch wide and 4-6 inches long.
7. Optional: Coat with seeds: If desired, you can roll the strips in sesame or poppy seeds for added flavour and presentation.

8. Bake: Place the strips on a baking sheet lined with parchment paper. Bake in the preheated oven for 12-15 minutes or until the cheese straws are golden and crisp.

9. Cool and serve: Allow the cheese straws to cool on the baking sheet for a few minutes before transferring them to a wire rack to cool completely. Once cooled, they are ready to be served.

Crudité Platters

Crudité platters are a fantastic addition to any party, offering a colourful and refreshing assortment of fresh vegetables paired with delicious dips. Here's a recipe to get you started:

Ingredients:

For the Crudité:
- Baby carrots
- Cherry tomatoes
- Cucumber, sliced
- Bell peppers (assorted colours), sliced
- Radishes, halved
- Broccoli florets
- Cauliflower florets
- Snap peas
- Celery sticks

For the Dips:
1. Classic Hummus:
   - 1 can (15 oz) chickpeas, drained and rinsed
   - 1/4 cup tahini
   - 2 cloves garlic, minced
   - 2 tablespoons lemon juice
   - 3 tablespoons olive oil
   - Salt and pepper to taste

2. Greek Yoghurt Dip:
   - 1 cup Greek yoghurt
   - 1 tablespoon fresh dill, chopped
   - 1 tablespoon fresh parsley, chopped
   - 1 clove garlic, minced
   - Salt and pepper to taste

3. Avocado Lime Dip:
   - 2 ripe avocados, mashed
   - 1 lime, juiced
   - 1/4 cup cilantro, chopped
   - Salt and pepper to taste

Instructions:
1. Prepare the Vegetables:
   - Wash and cut the vegetables into bite-sized pieces.
   - Arrange them on a large serving platter, leaving space for the dips.

2. Make the Dips:
   a. Classic Hummus:
      - In a food processor, combine chickpeas, tahini, garlic, lemon juice and olive oil.
      - Blend until smooth. Season with salt and pepper to taste.

   b. Greek Yoghurt Dip:
      - In a bowl, mix Greek yogurt, dill, parsley and minced garlic.
      - Season with salt and pepper.

   c. Avocado Lime Dip:
      - In a bowl, mash the avocados and add lime juice.
      - Stir in chopped cilantro and season with salt and pepper.

3. Assemble the Crudité Platter:
   - Arrange the dips in small bowls on the platter.
   - Fill the remaining space on the platter with the assorted fresh vegetables.

4. Serve:
   - Place the Crudité Platter in the centre of your party table.
   - Encourage guests to dip the vegetables into the various dips and enjoy!

Dips and Chips

Dips and chips like guacamole, salsa, hummus, or spinach and artichoke dip with tortilla chips, pita bread, or vegetable sticks for dipping (especially cucumber) are easier to make than you might think. Here are some ideas:

1. Guacamole:

Ingredients:
- 3 ripe avocados
- 1 small red onion, finely diced
- 1-2 tomatoes, diced
- 1 clove garlic, minced
- 1 lime, juiced
- Salt and pepper to taste
- Fresh cilantro, chopped (optional)

Instructions:
1. Cut the avocados in half and remove the pits. Scoop out the flesh into a bowl.
2. Mash the avocados with a fork or potato masher until smooth or slightly chunky, depending on your preference.
3. Add the diced red onion, tomatoes, minced garlic, lime juice, salt, pepper and cilantro (if using). Mix well.
4. Taste and adjust the seasoning if needed. Refrigerate for at least 30 minutes before serving.

2. Salsa:

Ingredients:
- 4-5 tomatoes, diced
- 1/2 red onion, finely chopped
- 1 jalapeño, seeds removed and finely diced
- 1/4 cup fresh cilantro, chopped
- 2 cloves garlic, minced
- 1 lime, juiced
- Salt and pepper to taste

Instructions:
1. Combine diced tomatoes, chopped red onion, jalapeño, cilantro, minced garlic, and lime juice in a bowl.
2. Mix well and season with salt and pepper to taste.
3. Refrigerate for at least 30 minutes before serving.

3. Hummus:

Ingredients:
- 1 can (15 oz) chickpeas, drained and rinsed
- 1/4 cup tahini
- 1 clove garlic, minced
- 2 tablespoons lemon juice
- 3 tablespoons olive oil
- Salt to taste
- Water (as needed for consistency)

Instructions:
1. In a food processor, combine chickpeas, tahini, garlic and lemon juice. Blend until smooth.
2. With the processor running, drizzle in the olive oil until well combined.
3. If the hummus is too thick, add water a tablespoon at a time until you reach your desired consistency.
4. Season with salt to taste. Refrigerate before serving.

4. Spinach and Artichoke Dip:

Ingredients:
- 1 package (10 oz) frozen chopped spinach, thawed and drained
- 1 can (14 oz) artichoke hearts, drained and chopped
- 1 cup mayonnaise
- 1 cup sour cream
- 1 cup grated Parmesan cheese
- 1 cup shredded mozzarella cheese
- 1 teaspoon garlic powder
- Salt and pepper to taste

Instructions:
1. Preheat the oven to 375°F (190°C).
2. In a bowl, combine spinach, artichoke hearts, mayonnaise, sour cream, Parmesan cheese, mozzarella cheese, garlic powder, salt and pepper.
3. Transfer the mixture to a baking dish and bake for about 25-30 minutes or until bubbly and golden brown on top.
4. Serve hot with tortilla chips, pita bread, or vegetable sticks.

Empanadas

Empanadas are a delicious and versatile dish that can be filled with various ingredients. Here's a basic empanadas recipe for a party, along with a flavourful beef filling.

Empanada Dough:

Ingredients:
- 3 cups all-purpose flour
- 1 teaspoon salt
- 1 cup unsalted butter, cold and cut into small pieces
- 1 egg
- 1/3 cup ice water

Instructions:
1. In a large mixing bowl, combine the flour and salt.
2. Add the cold, chopped butter to the flour mixture. Use your hands or a pastry cutter to incorporate the butter until the mixture resembles coarse crumbs.
3. In a separate small bowl, beat the egg and add it to the flour-butter mixture.
4. Gradually add the ice water, a little at a time, and mix until the dough comes together. Be careful not to overmix.
5. Divide the dough into two equal portions, shape them into discs, wrap in plastic, and refrigerate for at least 30 minutes.

Beef Filling:

Ingredients:
- 1 lb ground beef
- 1 small onion, finely chopped
- 2 cloves garlic, minced
- 1/2 cup bell pepper, diced
- 1/2 cup tomato sauce
- 1 teaspoon ground cumin
- 1 teaspoon smoked paprika
- Salt and pepper to taste
- 1/4 cup green olives, chopped
- 1/4 cup raisins

Instructions:
1. In a frying pan over medium heat, brown the ground beef.
2. Add the chopped onion, garlic and bell pepper. Cook until the vegetables are softened.
3. Stir in the tomato sauce, cumin, paprika, salt and pepper. Cook for an additional 5-7 minutes until the mixture thickens.
4. Remove the pan from heat and stir in the green olives and raisins. Allow the filling to cool.

Assembly and Baking:
1. Preheat the oven to 375°F (190°C).
2. Roll out the chilled dough on a floured surface to about 1/8-inch thickness.
3. Use a round cutter to cut out circles from the dough.
4. Place a spoonful of the beef filling in the centre of each dough circle.
5. Fold the dough over the filling, creating a half-moon shape, and press the edges to seal.
6. Place the empanadas on a baking sheet lined with parchment paper.
7. Optional: Beat an egg and brush it over the empanadas for a golden finish.
8. Bake for 20-25 minutes or until golden brown.
9. Allow the empanadas to cool slightly before serving.

These empanadas are sure to be a hit at your party! You can also prepare additional fillings, such as chicken, cheese, or vegetable, to offer a variety for your guests.

Miniature Bruschettas

Miniature bruschettas make for delightful party appetisers. They are not only delicious but also visually appealing. Feel free to customise the toppings based on your preferences or the preferences of your guests. They're sure to be a hit at your party!

Ingredients:
- Baguette or French bread
- Cherry tomatoes, diced
- Fresh basil leaves, chopped
- Mozzarella cheese, diced
- Olive oil

- Balsamic glaze (optional)
- Salt and pepper to taste

Instructions:
1. Preheat your oven to 375°F (190°C).
2. Cut the baguette or French bread into thin slices, about 1/2 inch thick. You can toast the slices for a few minutes in the oven to make them crispy.
3. Prepare the Toppings:
   - In a bowl, mix the diced cherry tomatoes, chopped fresh basil, and mozzarella cheese.
   - Drizzle olive oil over the mixture and toss gently to combine.
   - Season with salt and pepper to taste.

4. Assemble the Bruschettas:
   - Place the toasted baguette slices on a serving platter.
   - Spoon the tomato, basil and mozzarella mixture onto each slice.

5. Bake:
   - Place the assembled bruschettas in the preheated oven for about 5-7 minutes, or until the cheese is melted and bubbly.

6. Optional Finish:
   - If desired, drizzle balsamic glaze over the miniature bruschettas just before serving for an extra burst of flavour.

Miniature Tarts
Ingredients:

For the Crust:
- 1 1/4 cups all-purpose flour
- 1/2 cup unsalted butter, cold and cut into small cubes
- 1/4 teaspoon salt
- 2-3 tablespoons ice water

For the Filling:
- 1 cup milk
- 3 large eggs
- 1/2 cup shredded cheese (cheddar, Gruyere, or your favourite)
- 1/4 cup diced ham or cooked bacon (optional)
- 1/4 cup diced bell peppers (any colour)

- 2 tablespoons finely chopped onion
- 1 tablespoon chopped fresh herbs (such as parsley, chives, or thyme)
- Salt and pepper to taste

Instructions:

1. Prepare the Crust:
   - In a food processor, combine the flour, cold butter and salt. Pulse until the mixture resembles coarse crumbs.
   - Gradually add ice water, one tablespoon at a time, and pulse until the dough just comes together.
   - Form the dough into a ball, wrap it in plastic wrap and refrigerate for at least 30 minutes.

2. Preheat your oven to 375°F (190°C).
3. Roll out the dough. On a lightly floured surface, roll out the chilled dough to about 1/8-inch thickness. Using a round cookie cutter or a glass, cut out circles slightly larger than the cups of a miniature muffin tin.
4. Line the muffin tin. Press the dough circles into the cups of a miniature muffin tin, forming miniature tart shells.
5. In a bowl, whisk together the milk, eggs, cheese, ham or bacon (if using), bell peppers, onion, herbs, salt and pepper.
6. Spoon the filling into each tart shell, filling almost to the top.
7. Bake in the preheated oven for 15-20 minutes or until the tarts are set and the crust is golden brown.
8. Allow the miniature tarts to cool in the muffin tin for a few minutes before transferring them to a serving platter.

Sausage Rolls

Here's a simple recipe for classic delicious sausage rolls that you can serve at your party:

Ingredients:

For the filling:

- 1 pound (450g) ground pork sausage
- 1 small onion, finely chopped
- 2 cloves garlic, minced
- 1/2 cup breadcrumbs

- 1 teaspoon dried sage
- Salt and pepper to taste

For the pastry:
- 2 sheets of puff pastry (store-bought or homemade)
- 1 egg, beaten (for egg wash)

Instructions:
1. Preheat your oven to 400°F (200°C).
2. In a large mixing bowl, combine the ground pork sausage, chopped onion, minced garlic, breadcrumbs, dried sage, salt and pepper. Mix well until all the ingredients are evenly combined.
3. Roll out the puff pastry sheets on a lightly floured surface. If you're using store-bought puff pastry, follow the instructions on the package for thawing.
4. Divide the sausage mixture in half and spread it along the length of each puff pastry sheet, forming a log shape along one edge.
5. Roll the pastry over the sausage mixture to encase it completely. Seal the edges by pressing them together. Repeat the process for the second pastry sheet.
6. Cut each log into smaller sausage rolls, about 2 inches (5 cm) in length.
7. Place the sausage rolls on a baking sheet lined with parchment paper, leaving some space between each roll.
8. Brush the tops of the sausage rolls with beaten egg to give them a golden brown finish.
9. Bake in the preheated oven for 20-25 minutes or until the pastry is puffed and golden brown.
10. Allow the sausage rolls to cool slightly before serving. You can serve them as they are or with your favourite dipping sauce.

Shrimp Cocktail

Shrimp cocktail is a classic and elegant appetiser that's perfect for parties. Here's a simple recipe to make shrimp cocktail:

For the Shrimp:
- 1 pound large shrimp, peeled and deveined
- 1 tablespoon olive oil
- Salt and pepper to taste
- Lemon wedges for garnish

For the Cocktail Sauce:
- 1 cup ketchup
- 2 tablespoons horseradish (adjust to taste)
- 1 tablespoon Worcestershire sauce
- 1 tablespoon lemon juice
- 1 teaspoon hot sauce (optional)
- Salt and pepper to taste

Instructions:
1. Cook the Shrimp:
   - Preheat a large pot of water to boiling. Add a generous pinch of salt.
   - Add the shrimp to the boiling water and cook for 2-3 minutes, or until they turn pink and opaque.
   - Drain the shrimp and transfer them to an ice bath to cool quickly. Once cooled, pat them dry with paper towels.
   - In a bowl, toss the cooked shrimp with olive oil, salt and pepper.

2. Make the Cocktail Sauce:
   - In a bowl, combine ketchup, horseradish, Worcestershire sauce, lemon juice and hot sauce (if using). Mix well.
   - Season with salt and pepper to taste. Adjust the horseradish and hot sauce levels based on your preference for heat.

3. Serve:
   - Arrange individual glasses or small cups on a serving platter.
   - Place a dollop of cocktail sauce at the bottom of each glass.
   - Arrange the seasoned shrimp on top of the sauce.
   - Garnish with lemon wedges on the side.

4. Chill:
   - Cover and refrigerate the shrimp cocktail until ready to serve. It's best served chilled.

5. Serve:
   - Serve the shrimp cocktail glasses on a platter with additional lemon wedges on the side.
   - Optionally, you can garnish with fresh parsley or cilantro for a pop of colour.

Smoked Salmon Canapés

Smoked salmon canapés are elegant appetisers that are perfect for parties and gatherings.

Ingredients:
- 1 baguette, thinly sliced
- 8 oz (about 225g) smoked salmon, sliced
- 8 oz cream cheese, softened
- 1/4 cup red onion, finely chopped
- 2 tablespoons capers, drained and chopped
- 2 tablespoons fresh dill, chopped
- 1 tablespoon lemon juice
- Salt and pepper to taste

Instructions:
1. Prepare the baguette slices:
   - Preheat the oven to 350°F (175°C).
   - Place the baguette slices on a baking sheet and toast them in the oven until they are lightly golden and crispy. Keep an eye on them, as they can burn quickly. Remove from the oven and let them cool.

2. Make the Cream Cheese Mixture:
   - In a bowl, combine the softened cream cheese, chopped red onion, capers, fresh dill and lemon juice. Mix well until all the ingredients are evenly incorporated.

3. Season the Mixture:
   - Taste the cream cheese mixture and add salt and pepper according to your preference. The smoked salmon and capers can be salty, so be mindful of the seasoning.

4. Assemble the Canapés:
   - Once the baguette slices have cooled, spread a generous layer of the cream cheese mixture onto each slice.

5. Add Smoked Salmon:
   - Place a slice of smoked salmon on top of the cream cheese mixture on each baguette slice. You can fold the salmon or arrange it in a decorative way.

6. Garnish:
    - Garnish the canapés with additional fresh dill or lemon zest for a burst of flavour and a touch of colour.

7. Serve:
    - Arrange the smoked salmon canapés on a serving platter and serve them immediately. They can be enjoyed at room temperature.

You can also add a squeeze of lemon juice just before serving for an extra zing. These smoked salmon canapés are sure to impress your guests and make your party a hit!

Spanish Tortilla (Tortilla Española)

Making a Spanish tortilla (tortilla española) is a great idea for a party. It's a delicious and versatile dish that can be served as a main course or cut into smaller portions for appetisers. Here's a basic recipe for a traditional Spanish tortilla:

Ingredients:
- 6-8 medium-sized potatoes, peeled and thinly sliced
- 1 large onion, thinly sliced
- 6-8 eggs
- Salt and pepper to taste
- Olive oil for frying

Instructions:
1. Preparation:
    - Heat a generous amount of olive oil in a large frying pan over a medium heat.
    - Add the sliced potatoes and onions to the pan. Cook them until they are tender but not browned, stirring occasionally. This process may take around 10-15 minutes.

2. Drain:
    - Once the potatoes and onions are cooked, use a slotted spoon to transfer them to a large bowl. Allow any excess oil to drain off.

3. Beat Eggs:
    - In a separate bowl, beat the eggs and season with salt and pepper.

4. Combine:
   - Add the beaten eggs to the bowl with potatoes and onions. Mix well to ensure the potatoes and onions are evenly coated with the eggs.

5. Cooking the Tortilla:
   - Heat a couple of tablespoons of olive oil in a non-stick pan over medium heat.
   - Pour the potato and egg mixture into the pan, spreading it evenly. Cook for a few minutes until the edges start to set.

6. Flipping the Tortilla:
   - Once the edges are set, place a plate that is larger than the pan over the top. Invert the pan so that the tortilla is now on the plate.
   - Slide the tortilla back into the pan, uncooked side down. Cook for a few more minutes until the centre is set.

7. Serve:
   - Once the tortilla is cooked through and has a golden colour on both sides, remove it from the pan and let it cool for a few minutes.
   - Cut the tortilla into wedges or bite-sized pieces and serve warm.

Optional Additions:
- You can add diced bell peppers, chorizo or spinach to the potato and egg mixture for extra flavour.
- Serve with a side of aioli or a simple tomato sauce.

Spring Rolls

Spring rolls are not only tasty but also a great appetiser that your guests will love.

Ingredients:

For the Filling:
- 1 cup shredded cabbage
- 1 cup julienned carrots
- 1 cup bean sprouts
- 1 cup thinly sliced bell peppers (any colour)
- 1 cup cooked and shredded chicken or tofu (for a vegetarian option)
- 2 tablespoons soy sauce
- 1 tablespoon oyster sauce (optional)

- 1 tablespoon hoisin sauce
- 2 cloves garlic, minced
- 1 teaspoon ginger, grated
- 2 green onions, chopped
- 1 tablespoon sesame oil
- Salt and pepper to taste

For the Wrappers:
- Spring roll wrappers (available at most grocery stores)
- Water for sealing the wrappers

For Frying:
- Vegetable oil for deep frying

Instructions:
1. Prepare the Filling:
   - In a large bowl, combine shredded cabbage, julienned carrots, bean sprouts, sliced bell peppers and shredded chicken or tofu.
   - In a small bowl, mix soy sauce, oyster sauce, hoisin sauce, minced garlic, grated ginger, chopped green onions, sesame oil, salt and pepper. Pour this sauce over the vegetable mixture. Toss everything until well combined.

2. Assemble the Spring Rolls:
   - Place a spring roll wrapper on a clean surface with one corner pointing towards you.
   - Spoon a generous portion of the filling onto the wrapper.
   - Fold the corner closest to you over the filling, tucking it in slightly.
   - Fold in the sides, and then roll the spring roll away from you, sealing the edge with a little water.

3. Frying the Spring Rolls:
   - Heat vegetable oil in a deep fryer or a large, deep pan to 350°F (175°C).
   - Carefully place the spring rolls in the hot oil, a few at a time, and fry until they turn golden brown, turning occasionally for even cooking. This should take about 3-4 minutes per batch.
   - Remove the spring rolls with a slotted spoon and place them on a paper towel-lined plate to absorb excess oil.

4. Serve:
    - Serve the spring rolls with your favorite dipping sauce, such as sweet chili sauce or soy sauce with minced garlic and a splash of lime juice.

Sushi Rolls

Serving bite-sized sushi rolls with a selection of soy sauce, wasabi and pickled ginger makes for a delightful and interactive party dish. Here's a simple recipe for bite-sized sushi rolls:

Ingredients:
- Sushi rice
- Nori (seaweed) sheets
- Fresh fish (like tuna or salmon), thinly sliced
- Vegetables (cucumber, avocado, carrot), julienned
- Sesame seeds
- Soy sauce
- Wasabi
- Pickled ginger
- Bamboo sushi rolling mat
- Plastic wrap
- Rice vinegar
- Sugar
- Salt

Instructions:
1. Prepare Sushi Rice:
    - Rinse 2 cups of sushi rice under cold water until the water runs clear.
    - Cook the rice according to package instructions.
    - In a small bowl, mix 1/4 cup rice vinegar, 2 tablespoons sugar and 1 teaspoon salt. Gently fold this mixture into the cooked rice and let it cool.

2. Prepare Ingredients:
    - Slice the fresh fish and vegetables into thin, uniform strips.

3. Rolling the Sushi:
    - Place a bamboo sushi rolling mat on a flat surface and cover it with plastic wrap.

- Put a nori sheet, shiny side down, on the mat.
- Wet your hands and take a handful of sushi rice, spreading it evenly over the nori, leaving a small border at the top.
- Add strips of fish and vegetables on the rice.
- Sprinkle with sesame seeds.
- Roll the sushi tightly using the mat, sealing the edge with a bit of water.

4. Slice into Bite-Sized Pieces:
   - Use a sharp knife dipped in water to slice the rolled sushi into bite-sized pieces.

5. Serve:
   - Arrange the bite-sized sushi rolls on a platter.
   - Serve with small bowls of soy sauce, wasabi, and pickled ginger on the side.

6. Presentation Tips:
   - Garnish the platter with extra sesame seeds or chopped green onions for added flair.
   - Arrange the soy sauce, wasabi, and pickled ginger in small, attractive containers for easy dipping.

Encourage your guests to customise their bites with the soy sauce, a touch of wasabi for heat, and the pickled ginger for a palate cleanser.

Drinks

"All worries are less with wine."

Amit Kalantri

The drinks you serve can greatly influence the general atmosphere and enjoyment of your party. Some popular drink options to include are non-alcoholic drinks, including mocktails; alcoholic beverages, including craft and signature cocktails; and soft drinks. Providing plenty of water to keep your guests hydrated is essential, especially if alcohol is served. Servers bringing around intermittent trays of glasses of water and other soft drinks in between alcoholic beverages is always a good idea.

If alcohol is served, encourage responsible drinking and offer non-alcoholic options for designated drivers. Remember also to have appropriate glassware, garnishes, and ice on hand, and be sure to check the legal drinking age in your area and follow all applicable laws regarding the service of alcohol at your party.

Cocktails

Cocktails are magic and theatre in a glass. They were an American invention, first appearing in the early 19th century, although the British had been drinking punches composed of spirits, fruit juices and spices somewhat earlier.

Ultimately, any mixed alcoholic drink can be called a cocktail, although most involve spirits like vodka, gin and rum. You can find a cocktail for every mood and every occasion: sultry seductions, cheery celebrations, moments of reflection and melancholy, intimate conversations, glamourous galas and, of course parties!

Cocktails are a party drink – many people never drink them except at such celebrations. Trying new ones is half the fun. So is seeing a skilled barman, or 'mixologist' as many now like to be known, creating one. Unfortunately, preparing every cocktail from scratch, one at a time, takes far too long if you have a lot of guests, so batches of them must be made ahead of time. With just a little practice, you too can learn how to make a delectable cocktail to arouse the appetite or raise a toast while having tremendous fun. Half the fun of making cocktails is to do it in front of your guests. My tip is to practice beforehand so it looks as if you've been pouring them all your life.

If you're going to make knockout cocktails, it's always best to use top-quality ingredients, particularly in drinks such as Margaritas or Daiquiris, where the delicate balance of the drink can be affected if you don't use the freshest lime juice. As for equipment, cocktail shakers come in many different shapes and sizes. The Boston shaker is perhaps the best, half steel and half glass. A bar spoon is a must, teaspoon size, with a helter-skelter stem allowing for smooth pouring.

Shaken, stirred or straight up? Some of my closest friends swear that shaking is preferable to stirring. It can be a long, drawn-out debate. However, other people I know – within the hospitality industry – believe it's just the reverse. Choose the method which feels right for you. The point is to mix the drink and get it cold – either way, you don't want to overdo it. A drink that has been shaken too long will lose its concentration and end up resembling a Slush Puppie. If you prefer your drink to be stirred, you shouldn't stir too energetically, or you'll break up the ice.

The golden rule of good cocktail-making is to keep it simple. There are hundreds – perhaps thousands – of drink combinations, elaborate concoctions that include every imaginable extra of exotic mixer or fruit juice, and we would not attempt to supply the recipes for the many known cocktails. So, we will only feature a selection of classics you might consider serving at your party. These are classics that have passed the test of time.

In my opinion, most cocktails in the UK are served far too warm. Always have plenty of ice to hand (made from mineral water rather than tap water for a cleaner taste). Aim to frost glasses beforehand by leaving them in the fridge for at least an hour.

Unless you have a full-service bar with plenty of expert bar staff, choose one of two cocktails and serve assortments of those. Inevitably, cocktails containing sparkling wine, like Buck's Fizz (Mimosa in the USA) and Bellini, are less intoxicating than spirits-based cocktails – especially if the latter are made without strict measures of liquor.

Punch was traditionally *the* party drink, prepared in a vast bowl and ladled into glasses. It contained alcohol, fruit juice, sugar, water and perhaps something spicy like bitters.

One risk with cocktails is that mixers often disguise the taste of alcohol – so such drinks can be more intoxicating than guests are expecting. This especially applies at a private function when no measures are used when adding spirits.

I usually serve cocktails early in proceedings and then offer less strong drinks like wine and beer. This helps guests to pace their intake.

Remember, a good cocktail is only a couple of shakes away! Here are some of the best:

Aperol Spritz

The Aperol Spritz is a popular and refreshing Italian cocktail that has gained international acclaim. It's known for its vibrant orange colour and bittersweet flavour. Its simple recipe and appealing taste make it a favourite choice for those seeking a stylish and effervescent cocktail. The drink's popularity has also been boosted by successful endorsements and sponsorship of major sporting events that emphasise its vibrant colour and association with leisurely, convivial moments.

Ingredients:
- 3 parts Prosecco (about 90 ml)
- 2 parts Aperol (about 60 ml)
- 1 splash of soda water
- Ice
- Orange slice (for garnish)

Instructions:
1. Fill a large wine glass with ice cubes.
2. Pour in the Prosecco.
3. Add the Aperol.
4. Top with a splash of soda water.
5. Stir gently to combine the ingredients.
6. Garnish with an orange slice.

The Aperol Spritz has its origins in the Veneto region of Italy, particularly in the city of Venice. The cocktail's history can be traced back to the 1950s and 1960s. Aperol, the key ingredient in the drink, was created in 1919 by the Barbieri brothers in Padua, Italy. Aperol is an orange-flavoured aperitif with a distinctive bright orange hue.

The Aperol Spritz gained popularity as a light and refreshing drink, perfect for enjoying during the warm Italian summers. It became a symbol of the Italian lifestyle and is often associated with the concept of "aperitivo," a pre-dinner social ritual where people gather to enjoy drinks and snacks before the evening meal.

Bellini

The Bellini is a popular Italian cocktail that originated in Venice, Italy. It is a simple yet elegant drink, traditionally made with Prosecco and peach purée or peach nectar. Variations may include using different fruits, such as strawberries or raspberries, in place of peaches. The cocktail is known for its light, refreshing taste and beautiful peachy-pink colour. It has become a symbol of sophistication and is a must-try for those who appreciate simple yet delightful cocktails.

Ingredients:
- 2 ripe peaches (or you can use peach purée or peach nectar)
- 1 bottle of Prosecco, chilled

Instructions:
1. Peel and pit the peaches. Cut them into small pieces. You can also use frozen or canned peaches if fresh ones are not available. If using canned peaches, make sure they are in their natural juice and not in syrup.
2. Place the peach pieces in a blender and blend until you have a smooth purée.
3. Spoon 1-2 tablespoons of peach purée into the bottom of a chilled champagne flute. Slowly pour Prosecco over the purée until the glass is full.
4. Garnish the Bellini with a slice of fresh peach or a twist of lemon peel.
5. Gently stir the Bellini to mix the peach purée with the Prosecco before serving.

The Bellini's history dates back to the 1930s and is closely associated with the famous Harry's Bar in Venice. Giuseppe Cipriani, the founder of Harry's Bar, is credited with creating the Bellini. The cocktail was named after the Italian Renaissance painter Giovanni Bellini, who was known for his beautiful use of colours, particularly peach tones.

Cipriani created the Bellini in the mid-20th century, inspired by the beautiful peach colour in one of Bellini's paintings. The original Bellini recipe was made with a mix of white peach purée and Prosecco. Over the years, the drink gained international popularity and became a classic cocktail.

Bloody Mary

The Bloody Mary is a classic cocktail known for its savoury and spicy flavours. It has become a brunch and cocktail bar staple, celebrated for its bold flavours and customisable nature. Over time, countless variations and garnishes have been added to suit individual tastes.

Ingredients:
- 1 1/2 oz vodka
- 3 oz tomato juice
- 1/2 oz lemon juice
- Dash of Worcestershire sauce
- Dash of hot sauce (adjust to taste)
- Pinch of salt and pepper
- Celery salt (for rimming the glass, optional)
- Garnishes: Celery stalk, lemon wedge, olives, pickles, etc.

Instructions:
1. If desired, rim the glass with celery salt by moistening the rim with a lemon wedge and dipping it into the salt.
2. Fill the glass with ice cubes.
3. In a shaker, combine vodka, tomato juice, lemon juice, Worcestershire sauce, hot sauce, salt and pepper.
4. Shake well to combine the ingredients.
5. Strain the mixture into the prepared glass over ice.
6. Garnish with a celery stalk, lemon wedge, olives, or pickles.
7. Stir before sipping and adjust the seasoning to taste.

The exact origin of the Bloody Mary is somewhat unclear, and there are several theories about how it came to be. Here are a couple of popular stories:
1. Fernand Petiot (1920s): One widely accepted story attributes the creation of the Bloody Mary to Fernand Petiot, a bartender at Harry's New York Bar in Paris during the 1920s. The original recipe reportedly included equal parts of vodka and tomato juice, seasoned with salt, pepper, cayenne pepper and Worcestershire sauce.
2. George Jessel (1930s): Another theory credits the actor George Jessel with inventing the Bloody Mary. Jessel claimed that he created the cocktail in the 1930s as a hangover cure at the King Cole Bar in the St. Regis Hotel in New York City. He named it after his friend, Mary Brown Warburton, who was known as a bit of a wild character.

Buck's Fizz

The Buck's Fizz is a classic cocktail that's simple to make and refreshing to enjoy. It is traditionally made with orange juice and Champagne or sparkling wine. Over the years, the Buck's Fizz has become a popular choice for celebratory brunches, weddings, and other special occasions. It remains a timeless and elegant cocktail enjoyed by many for its simplicity and delightful flavour combination.

Ingredients:
- 1 part fresh orange juice
- 2 parts Champagne or sparkling wine
- Orange slice or twist, for garnish (optional)

Instructions:
1. Chill the Champagne or sparkling wine in the refrigerator before making the cocktail.
2. In a flute or champagne glass, pour the fresh orange juice.
3. Slowly pour the Champagne or sparkling wine over the orange juice.
4. Gently stir to mix the ingredients without losing the effervescence of the bubbly.
5. Optionally, garnish with a slice or twist of orange.

The Buck's Fizz cocktail is believed to have originated in the United Kingdom (one of the few classic cocktails to have done so), and its creation is often attributed to the bartender Pat McGarry. It is said to have been invented in the early 20th century, and the first mention of the Buck's Fizz appears in print in the excellent book *Harry's ABC of Mixing Cocktails* by Harry MacElhone, published in 1927.

The cocktail gained popularity as a morning or brunch drink due to its light and fruity nature. It's a variation of the classic Mimosa, which typically consists of equal parts orange juice and Champagne. The Buck's Fizz, with its higher ratio of Champagne to orange juice, provides a slightly stronger and more effervescent option.

Caipirinha

The Caipirinha is a popular Brazilian cocktail known for its refreshing and simple combination of ingredients. It is relatively cheap to make (in fact, they often say the cheapest cachaça is the best to use) and excellent for making large quantities if you have a lot of thirsty guests. It is the national drink of Brazil and is made with the country's signature distilled spirit, cachaça.

Ingredients:
- 2 ounces (60 ml) cachaça
- 1 lime, cut into wedges
- 2 teaspoons white sugar
- Ice cubes

Instructions:
1. Place the lime wedges in a glass.
2. Sprinkle the sugar over the lime wedges.
3. Using a muddler or the back of a spoon, muddle the lime and sugar together to extract the lime juice and dissolve the sugar.
4. Fill the glass with ice cubes.
5. Pour the cachaça over the ice.
6. Stir the mixture gently to combine the ingredients.
7. Garnish with a lime wheel on the rim of the glass.

The exact origin of the Caipirinha is somewhat debated, but it is generally believed to have originated in rural areas of Brazil. The cocktail is said to have humble beginnings, with sugarcane plantation workers using the available ingredients to create a refreshing drink. The word "caipirinha" is derived from "caipira," which refers to someone from the countryside.

Cachaça, the key ingredient in Caipirinha, is a distilled spirit made from fermented sugarcane juice. It has a distinct flavour that sets Caipirinha apart from other cocktails. The cocktail gained popularity in the 20th century, and it eventually became a symbol of Brazilian culture.

Cosmopolitan

The Cosmopolitan cocktail gained significant renewed fame due to its association with the hit television show "Sex and the City," where it was often featured. The combination of vodka, triple sec, cranberry juice and lime juice creates a refreshing and visually appealing cocktail that has become iconic in bars around the world.

Ingredients:
- 1 1/2 oz vodka
- 1 oz triple sec
- 1/2 oz cranberry juice

- 1/2 oz fresh lime juice
- Ice
- Orange twist or lime wheel for garnish

Instructions:
1. Place your martini glass in the freezer to chill while you prepare the cocktail.
2. Measure out the vodka, triple sec, cranberry juice, and fresh lime juice.
3. In a shaker, add the vodka, triple sec, cranberry juice, and fresh lime juice. Fill the shaker with ice.
4. Secure the shaker lid and shake the mixture vigorously for 15-20 seconds. This helps to chill the ingredients and mix them thoroughly.
5. Remove the martini glass from the freezer and strain the cocktail mixture into the glass, discarding the ice.
6. Garnish the Cosmopolitan with an orange twist or a lime wheel. To create an orange twist, use a vegetable peeler or a knife to cut a thin strip of orange peel, expressing the oils over the drink by giving it a twist.

The Cosmopolitan is a classic cocktail that gained popularity in the 1990s. While its exact origin is a matter of debate, it is widely believed to have been created by bartender Toby Cecchini in the early 1990s. Cecchini claims to have invented the drink while working at The Odeon in Manhattan.

However, another version of the cocktail's history attributes its creation to Cheryl Cook, a bartender in Miami who supposedly invented the drink in the late 1980s. According to Cook, she created the Cosmopolitan as a response to the growing popularity of flavoured vodkas.

Cuba Libre

The Cuba Libre is a classic cocktail associated with Cuban culture that originated in the early 20th century. The combination of rum, cola and lime created a refreshing beverage that appealed to many. It's a straightforward, simple and tasty drink that pays homage to a historical period – often linked to the Spanish-American War and the presence of American soldiers in Cuba – which symbolises the spirit of freedom.

Ingredients:
- 2 oz light rum
- 4 oz cola

- 1/2 oz fresh lime juice
- Lime wedge for garnish
- Ice cubes

Instructions:
1. Fill a highball glass with ice cubes.
2. Pour the rum over the ice.
3. Squeeze the lime juice into the glass.
4. Top with cola and gently stir.
5. Garnish with a lime wedge.

The Cuba Libre's history is intertwined with the Spanish-American War, which took place in 1898. Legend has it that the cocktail was created in Havana, Cuba, around this time. As the story goes, American soldiers stationed in Cuba during the war would mix local Cuban rum with cola. This mixture became known as "Cuba Libre," which means "Free Cuba" in Spanish, reflecting the desire for Cuba's independence.

Daiquiri

The Daiquiri's simple yet balanced combination of rum, lime and sweetness has made it a symbol of refreshing elegance and a testament to the enduring appeal of well-crafted, uncomplicated cocktails.

Ingredients:
- 2 oz white rum
- 1 oz fresh lime juice
- 3/4 oz simple syrup (1:1 ratio of water to sugar)
- Ice cubes
- Lime wheel or wedge, for garnish

Instructions:
1. Prepare simple syrups: in a saucepan, combine equal parts water and sugar. Heat over medium heat, stirring until the sugar dissolves. Allow it to cool before using.
2. Prepare cocktail by filling a cocktail shaker with ice cubes.
3. Add the white rum, fresh lime juice, and simple syrup to the shaker.
4. Shake the ingredients vigorously for 10-15 seconds to chill the mixture.
5. Strain the mixture into a chilled coupe or martini glass.
6. Garnish with a lime wheel or wedge on the rim of the glass.

The Daiquiri is a classic cocktail with its origins rooted in Cuba. Its creation is often attributed to an American mining engineer named Jennings Cox, who worked in the iron mines near the town of Daiquiri during the late 19th century. Legend has it that Cox concocted the drink as a refreshing solution to combat the tropical heat for himself and his colleagues.

The original Daiquiri was a simple mix of local ingredients – white rum, lime juice and sugar. The drink gained popularity over time and made its way to Havana, where it underwent some modifications. The El Floridita bar in Havana played a significant role in popularising the Daiquiri, especially the version with crushed ice and the addition of Maraschino liqueur.

Ernest Hemingway frequented El Floridita and had his own twist on the cocktail, known as the "Papa Doble," which included double the rum and no sugar.

Long Island Iced Tea

The Long Island Iced Tea is a popular and strong cocktail known for its combination of various spirits and mixers. Despite its name, it doesn't actually contain any tea.

Ingredients:
- 1/2 oz vodka
- 1/2 oz tequila
- 1/2 oz rum
- 1/2 oz gin
- 1/2 oz triple sec
- 3/4 oz sour mix
- 1 oz simple syrup
- Cola (to top off)
- Lemon wedge (for garnish)
- Ice cubes

Instructions:
- Fill a shaker with ice cubes.
- Add vodka, tequila, rum, gin, triple sec, sour mix and simple syrup to the shaker.
- Shake well to mix the ingredients.
- Strain the mixture into a highball glass filled with ice.
- Top off with cola, leaving some space at the top.

- Garnish with a lemon wedge.
- Stir gently before drinking.

The origin of the Long Island Iced Tea is a bit murky, with multiple claims to its invention. The cocktail's creation is often attributed to a contest held in the 1970s to create a new mixed drink using Triple Sec. One version of the story credits a bartender named Robert "Rosebud" Butt, who created the drink at the Oak Beach Inn in Long Island, New York, in the 1970s.

The Oak Beach Inn version of the Long Island Iced Tea had a slightly different recipe, including maple syrup instead of simple syrup. Over time, the recipe evolved and the drink became widely popular in various bars and restaurants. Despite its sweet and innocent name, the Long Island Iced Tea has a reputation for being a strong cocktail due to its mix of several different spirits.

Mai Tai

The Mai Tai is a classic cocktail that originated in the 1940s, gained popularity in the 1950s and has become a popular choice for those seeking a tropical and refreshing drink. The cocktail is associated with tiki culture and is often enjoyed in beach-themed or Polynesian-style settings.

Ingredients:
- 2 oz (60 ml) aged rum
- 3/4 oz (22.5 ml) fresh lime juice
- 1/2 oz (15 ml) orange liqueur (such as orange curaçao)
- 1/2 oz (15 ml) orgeat syrup
- 3/4 oz (22.5 ml) dark rum (float on top)
- Garnish: Mint sprig and lime wheel

Instructions:
1. Fill a shaker with ice.
2. Add the aged rum, fresh lime juice, orange liqueur, and orgeat syrup to the shaker.
3. Shake well until the mixture is chilled.
4. Strain the mixture into an old-fashioned glass filled with crushed ice.
5. Float the dark rum on top by pouring it gently over the back of a spoon.
6. Garnish with a mint sprig and a lime wheel.

The Mai Tai's origin is a subject of debate, but it is generally attributed to Victor "Trader Vic" Bergeron, who claimed to have created the cocktail in 1944 at his Trader Vic's restaurant in Oakland, California. The story goes that he made the drink for friends from Tahiti, and after tasting it, one of them exclaimed, "Maita'i roa ae!" which means "Out of this world—the best!" in Tahitian. This phrase eventually inspired the cocktail's name.

Another claim to the Mai Tai's invention comes from Donn Beach, the founder of Don the Beachcomber, a tiki-themed restaurant and bar. Beach's version, called the "Q.B. Cooler," is said to have inspired Trader Vic's creation.

Margarita

The Margarita is a classic cocktail that has become one of the most popular and enduring drinks around the world. It gained popularity in the United States during the 1940s and 1950s and remains a beloved cocktail with countless variations and adaptations. Timeless.

Ingredients:
- 2 oz (60 ml) Tequila
- 1 oz (30 ml) Triple sec or Cointreau
- 3/4 oz (22.5 ml) Freshly squeezed lime juice
- Ice
- Salt (for rimming the glass, optional)
- Lime wedge (for garnish)

Instructions:
1. If desired, moisten the rim of the glass with a lime wedge and dip it into salt to coat the rim. This step is optional and depends on personal preference.
2. In a shaker, combine the tequila, triple sec or Cointreau, and freshly squeezed lime juice Add ice.
3. Shake the ingredients well to chill the mixture.
4. Strain the mixture into the prepared glass over fresh ice.
5. Garnish with a lime wedge on the rim of the glass.

The origin of the Margarita is a bit murky, with several stories claiming to be the true birth of the cocktail. Here are a couple of popular theories:
1. Carlos "Danny" Herrera's Creation (1938): One story attributes the creation of the Margarita to Carlos "Danny" Herrera, a bartender at Rancho La Gloria in Tijuana, Mexico. As the story goes, in 1938, a

customer, a German ambassador's daughter, was allergic to all alcohol except tequila but found it too harsh. Herrera supposedly created the Margarita by combining tequila, lime and triple sec and serving it in a salt-rimmed glass.

2. Margarita Sames' Party (1948): Another popular story involves a socialite named Margarita Sames. In 1948, she claimed to have invented the cocktail during a house party in Acapulco. Sames combined tequila, Cointreau and lime juice, creating what she called the Margarita.

Martini

The Martini is a classic cocktail that has become an iconic symbol of sophistication and elegance. Whether served with a lemon twist or an olive, and whether made with gin or vodka, the Martini continues to be a timeless favourite among cocktail enthusiasts, with multiple variations that cater to individual preferences.

Ingredients:
- 2 oz (60 ml) gin
- 1/2 oz (15 ml) dry vermouth
- Ice cubes
- Lemon twist or olive, for garnish

Instructions:
1. Fill a mixing glass with ice cubes.
2. Pour the gin and dry vermouth into the mixing glass.
3. Stir the ingredients well for about 30 seconds to chill the mixture.
4. Strain the liquid into a chilled martini glass.
5. Garnish with a lemon twist or an olive.

Note: Some people prefer shaking a Martini instead of stirring, but traditionally, it is stirred to maintain clarity in the drink.

The origin of the Martini is unclear, and there are several theories about how it came to be. Here are a couple of popular theories:
1. Martinez Theory: One theory suggests that the Martini evolved from a drink called the Martinez, which was first mentioned in the 1860s. The Martinez was a combination of gin, sweet vermouth and orange bitters. Over time, the recipe evolved, and the sweet vermouth was gradually replaced with dry vermouth.

2. Gold Rush Theory: Another theory connects the Martini to the Gold Rush era in the United States. Miners were said to have invented the drink by mixing gin with fortified wine, and as the recipe evolved, dry vermouth was introduced.

The Martini gained widespread popularity during the early 20th century and became a symbol of elegance and sophistication. Its association with famous figures, such as James Bond ordering his Martinis "shaken, not stirred," further contributed to its iconic status.

Mojito

The Mojito is celebrated as a classic cocktail enjoyed worldwide, known for its refreshing and lively combination of mint, lime and rum. It has become a staple in bars and restaurants, especially during the warmer months, offering a taste of the Cuban sun and culture. The basic ingredients of the original Mojito included indigenous ingredients like sugarcane juice, lime, mint and a primitive form of rum. Over the years, the recipe has evolved, with variations featuring different types of rum and additional ingredients.

Ingredients:
- 2 oz (60 ml) white rum
- 1 oz (30 ml) fresh lime juice
- 2 teaspoons sugar (adjust to taste)
- 6-8 fresh mint leaves
- Soda water (club soda)
- Ice cubes
- Lime slices and mint sprigs for garnish

Instructions:
1. Start by muddling the mint leaves and sugar in a glass. Gently crush the mint to release its flavour.
2. Add fresh lime juice to the glass and continue to muddle to mix the ingredients.
3. Fill the glass with ice cubes.
4. Pour the white rum over the ice.
5. Top off the glass with soda water, leaving some space at the top for stirring.
6. Stir the ingredients gently to combine.
7. Garnish with a lime slice and a sprig of mint.

The Mojito is a traditional Cuban cocktail that dates back to the 16th century. Its exact origins are unclear, but it is widely believed to have been a favourite among pirates and sailors. The name "Mojito" is said to be derived from the Spanish word "mojo," which means to cast a spell.

The Mojito gained international popularity through Ernest Hemingway, who frequented La Bodeguita del Medio in Havana, Cuba. It is claimed that Hemingway declared La Bodeguita's Mojito as the best he ever tasted, contributing to the cocktail's global fame.

Negroni

The Negroni is a strong, classic cocktail with a rich history, known for its bittersweet and sophisticated flavour profile. It is one of only a handful of cocktails made by mixing more than one type of alcohol.

Ingredients:
- 1 oz (30 ml) Gin
- 1 oz (30 ml) Sweet Vermouth
- 1 oz (30 ml) Campari
- Orange slice or twist (for garnish)

Instructions:
1. Fill an old-fashioned glass (or a rocks glass) with ice cubes to chill the glass.
2. In a mixing glass, combine the gin, sweet vermouth and Campari.
3. Fill the mixing glass with ice and stir the ingredients well to chill the mixture. Stirring helps integrate the flavours without over-diluting the drink.
4. Strain the mixture into the prepared glass over fresh ice.
5. Garnish the cocktail with an orange slice or twist. The citrusy aroma complements the bittersweet flavours of the drink.

Tips:
- Adjust the ratio: The classic Negroni recipe uses equal parts gin, sweet vermouth and Campari. However, some people prefer slight adjustments to suit their taste preferences.
- Glassware: The Negroni is traditionally served in an old-fashioned glass over ice.

The Negroni is believed to have originated in Florence, Italy, in the early 20th century and is said to have been created in 1919 when Count Camillo

Negroni, a regular patron at Caffè Casoni in Florence, asked the bartender, Fosco Scarselli, to strengthen his Americano cocktail by adding gin instead of soda water. This modified version of the Americano became known as the "Negroni," and it quickly gained popularity.

The Negroni's popularity has endured for decades, and it has inspired countless variations and spin-offs. It's a cocktail appreciated by both novice and experienced cocktail enthusiasts for its bold and balanced flavours.

Pina Colada

Regardless of its exact origin, the Piña Colada has gained international popularity and become a symbol of tropical relaxation. It is a famous tropical cocktail known for its refreshing and sweet taste, often served in a chilled glass and garnished with tropical fruits.

Ingredients:
- 2 oz white rum
- 3 oz pineapple juice
- 1 oz coconut cream
- Ice cubes
- Pineapple slice and maraschino cherry for garnish (optional)

Instructions:
1. In a blender, combine the white rum, pineapple juice, and coconut cream.
2. Add a handful of ice cubes to the blender.
3. Blend the ingredients until smooth.
4. Pour the mixture into a chilled glass.
5. Garnish with a pineapple slice and a maraschino cherry if desired.

The Piña Colada's origin is often associated with Puerto Rico, where it is the national drink. The exact origin of the cocktail is debated, but it is widely believed to have been created in the 1950s or 1960s. There are two main stories attributing the creation of the Piña Colada to different locations and people.

1. Barrachina Story (San Juan, Puerto Rico):
   - One story credits Ramón "Monchito" Marrero, a bartender at the Caribe Hilton Hotel's Beachcomber Bar in San Juan, Puerto Rico. According to this version, Marrero created the Piña Colada

in 1954 after three months of experimentation. The drink was reportedly introduced to the public on August 15, 1954.

2. Bacardi Story (Caguas, Puerto Rico):
   - Another story attributes the creation of the Piña Colada to a different Puerto Rican bartender, Ramón Portas Mingot. He is said to have made the drink in the 1960s at the Barrachina Restaurant in Old San Juan. This version of the story claims that the recipe was later acquired by Bacardi, and the drink gained popularity from there.

Punch

Punch remains a versatile and communal drink that can be enjoyed on various occasions. Recipes continue to evolve, and modern variations often include a wide range of ingredients, such as different spirits, fruit juices and flavoured syrups. It's perfect for large parties!

Ingredients:
- 1 cup of lemon juice
- 1 cup of simple syrup (equal parts sugar and water, dissolved together)
- 2 cups of strong black tea, chilled
- 2 cups of dark rum
- 1 cup of brandy
- 1 lemon, thinly sliced
- 1 orange, thinly sliced
- Ice cubes
- Nutmeg (for garnish)

Instructions:
1. In a punch bowl, combine the lemon juice, simple syrup, black tea, dark rum and brandy.
2. Add the lemon and orange slices to the mixture.
3. Refrigerate the punch for at least an hour to allow the flavours to meld.
4. Just before serving, add ice cubes to the punch bowl.
5. Grate fresh nutmeg over the top for garnish.

The "Punch" cocktail has a rich history dating back to the 17th century, originating from India and making its way to England. The name "punch" is believed to be derived from the Hindi word "panch," meaning five, which refers to the traditional five ingredients used in the original punch recipes. These ingredients typically included spirits, citrus, sugar, water and spices.

- Origins in India: Punch is believed to have originated in India, where sailors and employees of the British East India Company encountered a local beverage known as "paantsch." This concoction consisted of five key ingredients: alcohol, sugar, lemon, water and tea or spices.
- Introduction to England: The concept of punch was introduced to England in the early 17th century by sailors and traders. As it made its way to England, the recipe evolved, incorporating ingredients that were more readily available in Europe.
- Popularity in the 18th Century: Punch became extremely popular in the 18th century, particularly at social gatherings and parties. It was often served in large bowls and became a symbol of conviviality and hospitality.
- Colonial America: Punch also gained popularity in colonial America, where it became a staple at social events and gatherings.

Sangria

Sangria is a refreshing and flavourful cocktail which gained international popularity in the mid-20th century, particularly in the United States and other parts of Europe. Its vibrant colours, refreshing taste, and customisable nature make it a favourite for summer parties and gatherings. Although there are countless variations and recipes for Sangria, it is typically made with red wine, fruit juices, soda water, fruit slices and sometimes liqueurs.

Ingredients:
- 1 bottle of red wine (750 ml)
- 1 orange, thinly sliced
- 1 lemon, thinly sliced
- 2 tablespoons sugar (adjust to taste)
- 1 shot of brandy or orange liqueur (optional)
- 1 cup orange juice
- 1 cup soda water or club soda
- Ice cubes
- Additional fruits like berries, peaches, or apples (optional)

Instructions:
1. In a large pitcher, combine the red wine, orange slices, lemon slices and sugar. Stir well until the sugar is dissolved.
2. If you're using brandy or orange liqueur, add it to the pitcher and stir.
3. Add the orange juice and soda water, mixing gently.
4. Taste the Sangria and adjust the sweetness by adding more sugar if needed.
5. Refrigerate the Sangria for at least two hours or preferably overnight to allow the flavours to meld.
6. Before serving, add ice cubes to the pitcher and stir gently.
7. Serve the Sangria in glasses, making sure to include some fruit slices in each glass.

Sangria's origins can be traced back to Spain, where it has been enjoyed for centuries. The word "sangria" is derived from the Spanish word "sangre," which means blood, referring to the traditional red wine base of the drink. While the exact origins are unclear, Sangria likely developed as a way to make wine more palatable and enjoyable, especially during hot weather.

In Spain, Sangria is often associated with social gatherings and celebrations. It is a versatile drink that can be adapted to suit personal preferences, with variations using white wine or sparkling wine instead of red, and different fruits and spirits added.

Screwdriver

The Screwdriver is a classic cocktail that's simple to make and quite popular. It's essentially a mix of vodka and orange juice. The Screwdriver has become a staple in bars and homes worldwide, making it a timeless and easy-to-enjoy cocktail.

Ingredients:
- 2 oz (60 ml) vodka
- 4 oz (120 ml) orange juice
- Ice cubes
- Orange slice or twist (for garnish)

Instructions:
1. Fill a highball glass with ice cubes.
2. Pour the vodka over the ice.
3. Add the orange juice.

4. Stir gently to combine.
5. Garnish with an orange slice or twist.

One famous story attributes its creation to American engineers in the Middle East during the mid-20th century. The story goes that these engineers would stir their drinks with screwdrivers when no other utensils were available, leading to the birth of the cocktail.

Another tale suggests that the cocktail became popular in the United States during the 1940s and 1950s. It is said that it was named the "Screwdriver" because bartenders would use screwdrivers to mix the drink. The simplicity of the cocktail likely contributed to its widespread adoption.

Sea Breeze

A versatile cocktail that can be customised to suit different taste preferences, the Sea Breeze is a classic cocktail that gained popularity in the 1970s and 1980s. It is known for its refreshing and fruity flavour. The drink typically consists of vodka, cranberry juice and grapefruit juice. Its simplicity and balance of sweet, citrusy and tart flavours contribute to its enduring popularity. It is often enjoyed in warm weather at beachside bars, pool parties and other summer gatherings.

Ingredients:
- 1 1/2 oz vodka
- 4 oz cranberry juice
- 1 oz grapefruit juice
- Ice
- Grapefruit slice or wedge (for garnish)

Instructions:
1. Fill a shaker with ice cubes.
2. Pour the vodka into the shaker.
3. Add the cranberry juice to the shaker.
4. Add the grapefruit juice to the shaker.
5. Put the lid on the shaker and shake the mixture well to chill the ingredients.
6. Strain the mixture into a highball glass filled with ice cubes.
7. Garnish the drink with a grapefruit slice or wedge.
8. Optional: You can also use a stirrer or a straw to mix the ingredients in the glass before sipping.

The Sea Breeze is believed to have originated in the 1920s or 1930s. Like many classic cocktails, its precise origins are a bit unclear, but it likely emerged during the era of Prohibition in the United States.

The Sea Breeze is part of a family of cocktails that includes the Cape Codder and the Bay Breeze. All three cocktails share the combination of vodka and cranberry juice, but the Sea Breeze distinguishes itself by adding grapefruit juice, giving it a unique and more complex flavour profile.

Tequila Sunrise

The Tequila Sunrise is known for its visually striking appearance, with the gradient of colours resembling a sunrise. It has remained a popular cocktail, enjoyed for its fruity and refreshing taste, making it a staple at many bars and gatherings.

Ingredients:
- 2 oz (60 ml) Tequila
- 4 oz (120 ml) Orange juice
- 1/2 oz (15 ml) Grenadine
- Ice cubes
- Orange slice and maraschino cherry for garnish (optional)

Instructions:
1. Fill a highball glass with ice cubes.
2. Pour the tequila and orange juice into the glass and stir well.
3. Slowly pour the grenadine over the back of a spoon or by drizzling it down the side of the glass, allowing it to settle at the bottom.
4. Do not stir after adding the grenadine; let it settle to create the gradient effect.
5. Garnish with an orange slice and a maraschino cherry if desired.
6. Serve and enjoy!

The Tequila Sunrise is believed to have originated in the 1930s or 1940s, and it gained popularity in the 1970s. There are various claims to its creation, but one commonly accepted story attributes it to Gene Sulit, a bartender at the Arizona Biltmore Hotel in Phoenix. He is said to have created the cocktail in the 1930s and named it after the beautiful sunrise seen in the Arizona desert.

The cocktail gained widespread fame when it was featured in the 1973 movie *The Tequila Sunrise*, starring Mel Gibson and Michelle Pfeiffer. The film's association with the cocktail contributed to its popularity, and it became a fashionable drink during the 1970s and 1980s.

White Russian

The White Russian is a simple and delicious cocktail enjoyed by many for its smooth and indulgent flavour that gained popularity in the 1960s and is known for its creamy and sweet taste.

Ingredients:
- 2 oz (60 ml) vodka
- 1 oz (30 ml) coffee liqueur (such as Kahlúa)
- 1 oz (30 ml) heavy cream or milk
- Ice cubes

Instructions:
1. Fill a rocks glass with ice cubes.
2. Pour the vodka and coffee liqueur over the ice.
3. Gently float the heavy cream or milk on top by pouring it over the back of a spoon or by using a cocktail shaker with a gentle pour.
4. Stir gently before drinking to combine the ingredients.

Optional:
- You can garnish with a sprinkle of nutmeg or cocoa powder on top.

The White Russian is a variation of the Black Russian, which is a cocktail made with vodka and coffee liqueur. The addition of cream or milk to create the White Russian is said to have originated in the 1960s. The exact history of the White Russian is unclear, but it is believed to have gained popularity in the United States during that era. Some sources credit the creation of the White Russian to a Belgian bartender named Gustave Tops, who is said to have created the cocktail in the 1950s at the Hotel Metropole in Brussels.

The cocktail became widely known in the 1998 film *The Big Lebowski*, where the main character, The Dude, played by Jeff Bridges, is a fan of the drink. The White Russian has since become somewhat iconic, associated with the laid-back and easy-going attitude of The Dude.

Mocktails

Roy Rogers

The Roy Rogers is a non-alcoholic cocktail named after the famous American singer and actor Roy Rogers. It's a simple and refreshing drink, popular with those who enjoy the taste of cola.

Ingredients:
- 1/2 oz grenadine syrup
- Cola (Coca-Cola or any cola of your choice)
- Maraschino cherry (for garnish)
- Ice cubes

Instructions:
1. Fill a tall glass with ice cubes.
2. Pour the grenadine syrup over the ice.
3. Fill the glass with cola, leaving some space at the top.
4. Stir gently to mix the grenadine and cola.
5. Garnish with a maraschino cherry.

The Roy Rogers cocktail is similar to a Shirley Temple, another popular non-alcoholic drink, but instead of ginger ale or lemon-lime soda, it uses cola. As for the history, the cocktail is named after Roy Rogers, who was a popular singing cowboy and actor in the 1940s and 1950s who didn't drink alcohol. Partly because of this, he became a cultural icon, particularly among young audiences. The drink was likely created as a marketing or promotional tie-in with Rogers' image, much like the Shirley Temple, named after the famous child actress.

Shirley Temple

The Shirley Temple is a non-alcoholic cocktail that has been a popular choice for decades, especially among children and those who don't consume alcohol. It is known for its sweet and fruity flavour.

Ingredients:
- 1/2 cup ginger ale
- 1/2 cup lemon-lime soda (such as Sprite or 7UP)
- 1 dash grenadine syrup
- Maraschino cherry and orange slice for garnish
- Ice cubes

Instructions:
1. Fill a glass with ice cubes.
2. Pour the ginger ale and lemon-lime soda into the glass.
3. Add a dash of grenadine syrup to create the signature pink colour.
4. Stir gently to mix the ingredients.
5. Garnish with a maraschino cherry and an orange slice.
6. Optionally, you can stir the drink again before serving.

The Shirley Temple cocktail was named after the famous child actress Shirley Temple, who was a Hollywood star in the 1930s. The drink is believed to have been created in the 1930s or 1940s, and its origin is often attributed to a bartender at the Brown Derby restaurant in Hollywood. The story goes that Shirley Temple used to visit the restaurant with her parents, and the bartender created the non-alcoholic drink in her honour.

The original recipe might have varied, but it typically includes ginger ale, a lemon-lime soda, and a splash of grenadine syrup. The result is a sweet, fizzing and visually appealing beverage that has since become a classic mocktail enjoyed by people of all ages. The Shirley Temple has maintained its popularity over the years and is still commonly served in restaurants and at events as a delightful non-alcoholic option.

Wine and beer

An excellent party should serve cocktails, wine and beer. This means planning is more complicated, and perhaps the cost slightly greater – but offering your guests a proper choice is civilised and generous.

If you serve beer, I recommend one lager and one ale. Ideally, choose a few local craft beers rather than the prominent brands. You might also supply a cider. In a perfect world, you would buy them on a sale or return basis so that any unused drink can be returned for a refund. If you are holding your party in a venue, they will supply their own selection of drinks. Party caterers can usually source a good range of wines and beers.

Many beer drinkers don't mind drinking directly from a bottle or can – but if you are hosting a classy evening, you should pour the beer into a glass. I'd suggest providing as much variety of beer as you can; light lager, hoppy IPAs, wheat beers and malty stouts. Non-alcoholic or low-alcohol beer has become increasingly popular in bars and restaurants of late, which is great. I'm thrilled to see this. Some popular and well-regarded non-alcoholic beer options include:

1. Heineken 0.0: Heineken's non-alcoholic version has gained popularity for its crisp and refreshing taste, resembling the original beer.
2. Clausthaler Original: This German brand is known for its high-quality, non-alcoholic beer with a malty flavour and balanced bitterness.
3. Athletic Brewing Co. Upside Dawn Golden Ale: Athletic Brewing specialises in craft non-alcoholic beers, and their Upside Dawn Golden Ale is well-received for its light and easy-drinking profile.
4. Beck's Blue: Another popular non-alcoholic option, Beck's Blue is a non-alcoholic version of the well-known German beer, Beck's. It has a light and malt-forward taste.
5. Bravus Brewing Co. Oatmeal Stout: For those who enjoy darker beers, Bravus Brewing Co. offers a non-alcoholic Oatmeal Stout that has received positive reviews for its rich and robust flavour.
6. Partake Brewing IPA: Partake Brewing is known for its non-alcoholic craft beers, and their IPA is appreciated by those who enjoy the hoppy and flavourful characteristics of traditional IPAs.
7. Lucky Saint 0.5% Alcohol Free Superior Unfiltered Lager: Popular lager made with four natural ingredients: Pilsner Malt, Hallertau Hops, spring water and classic lager yeast. This combination of ingredients and a unique brewing process creates a full-bodied lager with a refreshing citrus hop finish.

Wine is frequently the most popular beverage at a party. Again, offer red and white – and perhaps even rose – to please all tastes. Drinks like white wine and lager must be kept chilled, so use buckets or bowls of ice to store them in.

Wine specialists like Majestic Wine do all sorts of deals for customers holding a party, like complimentary glass hire (you do have to pay for breakages), free drink delivery if you order over £75 worth of drink, free chiller bins, and sale or return of drinks under certain terms. They sell hundreds of wines at reasonable prices – especially by the crate.

Majestic also has a rather ingenious drink calculator on their website – suggesting that, on average, you need one glass of wine per person for a short cocktail party, two for a more extended event, and three if there's a meal.

As ever, you need to order in advance to be sure they can reserve glasses, buckets and enough of your preferred wine for your grand event.

As for non-alcoholic wine, I've yet to find a supplier who has really hit this on the head (considering the delicacies of sweetness, acidity and flavour compared to beer makes this a much more difficult market to get right). But new start-ups are trying, which I applaud, and we're still in the early days. Here are some popular non-alcoholic wine options:

1. Ariel Cabernet Sauvignon (Non-Alcoholic): Ariel is a well-known brand offering non-alcoholic wines. Their Cabernet Sauvignon is often praised for its rich flavour and resemblance to traditional red wine.

2. Fre Brut Sparkling Non-Alcoholic Wine: This sparkling wine is known for its crisp taste and is a popular choice for those who enjoy the effervescence of traditional sparkling wines.

3. Sutter Home Fre White Zinfandel: Sutter Home offers a range of non-alcoholic wines, and their White Zinfandel is often appreciated for its fruity and refreshing taste.

4. Torres Natureo Rosé: Torres is a renowned winery, and its Natureo Rosé is a non-alcoholic option well-regarded for its delicate and fruity profile.

5. St. Regis De-Alcoholised Cabernet Sauvignon: This non-alcoholic Cabernet Sauvignon is known for its smooth and full-bodied taste, resembling traditional red wine.

6. Giesen 0% Sauvignon Blanc: Giesen, a winery from New Zealand, produces a non-alcoholic Sauvignon Blanc that has received positive feedback for its crisp and vibrant characteristics.

7. Seedlip: While not wine, Seedlip offers non-alcoholic distilled spirits that can be used to create sophisticated mocktails. They have various flavours, such as Spice 94 and Garden 108.

Chapter 11

Dinner Parties

"All human history attests
That happiness for man – the hungry sinner! –
Since Eve ate apples, much depends on dinner."

Lord Byron

Dinner parties are the easiest and sometimes the most fraught social occasions to host. They can be simpler than larger events because the guest list is typically much shorter than for a party with dancing and so forth. But at a dinner party, your guests are seated together for perhaps a few hours – and if you are the chef, they are eating your cooking. Mistakes are more intense in such a setting than at a big bash.

Dinner parties go in and out of fashion. I have an excellent *Esquire Handbook for Hosts*, first published in 1954. It's supposedly written for 'The Sophisticated Man'. It is really a guide to holding a dinner party – rather than other social functions. In previous eras, eating out with friends at restaurants was not as ubiquitous as it is now – the vast array of eating establishments available in the 2020s means people are much less likely to cook for friends at home in a semi-formal way.

However, going to a restaurant has disadvantages over hosting a dinner party at home. It will likely be more expensive – especially if you are paying for everyone. It will also be a somewhat more perfunctory affair, particularly if you book a table rather than a private room. While there might appear more food and drink choices than in your home, there will be no opportunity to delight your friends with your piece de resistance on the cooking front.

Preparing a meal for friends in your home is an intimate and unique gesture. Sharing your favourite dishes with your favourite people should be a great pleasure. But it takes effort. You have to choose a date and invite guests, buy ingredients and cook them, and after the meal, once your guests have left, you have to tidy up.

Dinner parties can be elaborate affairs, with formal printed invitations and professional caterers. Or they can be casual suppers around the kitchen table, organised with minimal fuss. The latter are often more fun– relaxed, less stuffy – and somehow more authentic.

But the dinner served is different from cooking for those you live with. If you have invited people around for an evening meal, you cannot simply get away with ordering takeaway pizza. Nevertheless, the occasion should not feel like work. If you hate cooking, I suggest you only host dinner parties in one of the private dining rooms that many thousands of pubs and restaurants make available for such gatherings – or hire a chef.

Of course, dining in a restaurant is more expensive – and much less personal. Ultimately, nothing compares to the privacy and warmth of your kitchen or dining room. But often, hosts are so busy cooking and serving food and then clearing up at home that they hardly have time to relish the company of their guests. Thus, the entire purpose of the get-together is defeated.

The menu for the meal should be to your taste. Do not slavishly follow fashion or be cajoled into serving food you don't like by a pushy foodie or friend. If you are cooking, I suggest you prepare dishes you feel very confident about preparing well – testing new recipes at a dinner party is a dangerous undertaking. Remember – delicious food doesn't have to be pretentious.

Ultimately, I tend to favour perennial favourites – classic comfort food – most of which can be prepared in advance. Be sure to cook generous portions – running out of food is a serious faux pas.

Only a main course is necessary for a simple affair, with a dessert to follow. For a more elaborate evening, a starter would be usual. Again, I would encourage you to serve unfussy food rather than exotic dishes – but do source good ingredients. Do a cold starter, which can be prepared in advance, or perhaps something that requires heating – soup, perhaps. Similarly, dessert should be uncomplicated – a cake from GAIL's Bakery or top-quality ice cream and fruit.

You should probably only invite close friends to a dinner party – or those you hope will become good friends. The custom is that partners are separated, which makes good sense since they see each other all the time.

Many hosts also arrange the seating by alternating the sexes. I feel this habit is rather old-fashioned and doesn't work if there is an unequal balance of men and women.

How big should a dinner party be? It depends on your culinary skills and the size of your kitchen or dining room. You can be more ambitious if you go to the trouble and expense of getting the meal catered. If you are cooking using domestic facilities at home, somewhere between six and twelve seated for supper is manageable.

It is worth thinking about the seating plans in advance and drawing up a *placement* so the right, electric combinations of people can spark general merriment. Impromptu seating can lead to awkward juxtapositions. You can write individual place cards as a special touch.

Remember to ask your guests in advance if they have particular dietary requirements. So many people have allergies or are vegetarian or vegan – failure to consider this is likely to lead to unhappiness.

Most evenings start with drinks, canapes, nibbles, or hor d'oeuvres before the meal. Americans tend to call such light snacks 'appetisers'. These preprandial mouthfuls are usually drunk and eaten in the sitting room before the main meal at a dining table elsewhere. They should whet the appetite but not satisfy people's hunger entirely – otherwise, they will not eat the food to come at dinner.

Typically, guests will be offered a cocktail, champagne, or sparkling wine before the meal. If you have a full range of spirits and mixers, you can provide a range of cocktails; if not, perhaps gin or vodka and tonic water and tomato juice will do.

Often, hosts phrase a dinner invitation, thus: '7 for 7:30 dinner'. This means there are drinks beforehand, but the intention is to serve food at 7:30pm. It provides a grace period when guests can turn up but warns that they should not be later than 7:30pm.

Conversation at a typical dinner party is usually a free-for-all. The table might participate in one joint conversation – particularly if there are only six people at a round table or guests might talk to the person sitting next to them. If that is the order of the day, ensure you give equal attention to those sitting on both your left and right. In such circumstances, hosts usually don't interfere.

However, some hosts encourage more serious debate and guide the group towards a communal chat about a particular topic. My wife and I once attended a large dinner party at a very wealthy man's house. He insisted that each guest introduce themselves to the gathering. It almost felt as if we were at a business conference. Later, he asked that we all contribute to a meaningful discussion on a weighty political subject. It was not a fun evening – although it was undeniably memorable!

Of course, more profound subjects tend to be more stimulating. I don't enjoy a dinner party discussing summer holidays, sports and the latest TV drama. But what should one talk about: Gossip? Personal tragedies? Children? Pets? The food? Or perhaps weightier matters…

Inevitably, the subjects that are often described as off-limits – like politics and religion – can be the ones that excite the most passion. Philosophical issues often elicit more thoughtful exchanges. There is no harm in thinking of a few subjects in advance to introduce if it feels apt. But don't force it – as long as your guests are having a good time, you are doing your job as host.

None of this is to say that witty anecdotes, jokes and other light-hearted banter aren't welcome. Excellent storytellers are always sought-after guests. Inevitably, the balance of conversation depends upon the selection of diners – and, indeed, how much alcohol has been consumed!

Guests should never look at mobile phones during a dinner party, and hosts should set an example and behave similarly. I sometimes see groups eating out, and everyone is simultaneously staring at their digital devices in silence. It is a pathetic scene. When friends and family are sitting in front of you, give them your entire attention – do not get distracted by trivial social media posts or inconsequential texts. I hope everyone at your party puts their phone away and refrains from looking at them for the entire evening – because they are so captivated by the company.

The lockdowns were a powerful reminder that meeting face-to-face for a thought-provoking discussion is a sublime activity that is hard to beat. Gatherings were illegal for many months in 2020 and 2021 owing to government restrictions, so we all have a lot of socialising to catch up on. Dinner parties are the best way ever invented to achieve exhilarating conversations in a civilised and intimate manner.

Chapter 12

Stag and Hen Parties

Stag parties (called Bachelor Parties in the US) are male-only gatherings thrown in honour of the groom just before his wedding. Traditionally, they were a black-tie supper held on the eve of the marriage day. Now, they have metastasised into incredibly elaborate affairs, frequently involving a long weekend away at a foreign location. The attendees are usually the groom, his best man, ushers and possibly close male relatives, such as the groom's father and brothers.

The roots of the stag stretch back to Ancient Greece when a group of men enjoyed a night of exuberance and feasting just before one was about to become betrothed. This was meant to signify a final evening of freedom from the commitments to his wife-to-be and the responsibilities of being a good husband. Alcohol has always played a prominent part in such celebrations, and little has changed. My experience of stag parties is that they are, at heart, an excuse for men to get very drunk indeed. The additional aim is to embarrass the groom when they are much the worse for wear.

I can recall one debased stag I attended many years ago, held at the rather grand Army & Navy Club in St James's Square, London. Towards the end of dinner, the very inebriated groom was persuaded to take off all his clothes (he was something of an exhibitionist). Then the groomsmen ambushed him and pushed him onto the balcony of the first-floor dining room and locked the doors, leaving him stranded there – naked. The gathering then left the dining room for the bar downstairs. A very British boys' boarding school sort of prank, I thought.

After a while, a few of us sneaked back from the bar and let him back in to retrieve his clothes. We felt the joke had turned stale and was becoming cruel. Such mischief is typical fare for a stag party. Some japes are recounted in the Best Man's speech at the subsequent wedding.

Stag parties are big business, and plenty of organisers specialise in booking activities, from axe throwing to car smashing to archery to a 'prison experience'. If you are the host tasked with organising this type of stag party, you should consult carefully with the other attendees to be sure your plans are within their budget range – and deemed fun.

Meanwhile, many grooms and best men now insist that a stag party must be a whole weekend away in a foreign city. Favourite destinations include boisterous places like Berlin, Las Vegas, Budapest, Prague and Amsterdam. All have a wild nightlife, from bierkellers to discotheques to casinos, and most offer an assortment of exotic entertainment for those who enjoy more risqué excursions.

Hen Parties are all-female gatherings held before a wedding to celebrate the bride-to-be's final days of freedom. The Americans call them bachelorette parties. The attendees are usually the bridesmaids – close friends and perhaps a few female family members. They are an opportunity for women to bond, let their hair down and have some fun, be it raucous or calm. Hen parties are either a single evening's entertainment or an entire weekend's festivities. The choice depends on the guests' budgets and their appetite for such frolics. Often, there is a theme to the affair – nostalgia, *Barbie*, *Mamma Mia*, or whatever is the bride's favourite movie.

While music, dancing and alcohol are usually a big part of a hen party, the organised activities tend to be somewhat more restrained than the goings on at a stag do. So, a hen party might include a manicure, a cookery class, a visit to a spa, yoga or even a baking class. But it could also include axe throwing, go-karting, a helicopter ride, or a bottomless brunch – and a bar crawl is very likely to feature! Since there are typically only ten or fewer ladies in a hen group, it's important that they all get on; if there are ancient feuds simmering away between people, then it's better that such enemies are excluded.

The cost of the affair needs to be calculated beforehand – it needs to be affordable for all the guests. It is intolerable to arrange a lavish weekend and then impose the cost on each guest, with the implication that anyone who doesn't attend isn't really a close friend of the bride. There are an infinite number of inexpensive and enjoyable ways for a bunch of people to have a lively time – even if it means a movie night at someone's house. The real joy is the company of other people; after all, singing and dancing together are free.

Someone must take charge of the Hen party – possibly the bride chooses who, or it might be that their very best friend volunteers herself for the task. It can be a lot of work and means juggling various competing interests. There will always be conflicts over dates, destinations, activities and so forth. The master of ceremonies needs to be a diplomat but also capable of making executive decisions. Often, the details of the Hen are kept secret from the bride, so everything except the date is a surprise to her, which can add to the pleasure of the event.

Because hen parties can involve a lot of booze, it makes sense for at least some of the entourage to remain reasonably sober to ensure no one gets in any trouble or drinks to excess and falls ill. As ever, balance is the key: the occasion must be exuberant and perhaps mildly dissolute but not dangerous.

In theory, each bride should only ever have one hen party in her honour; while a small amount of embarrassment might be in order, it is important that nothing happens that the guests truly regret afterwards – especially since these days everything is recorded on someone's smartphone.

Chapter 13

The Wedding Party

I have been invited to and have been involved in many weddings. Fortunately, I've only been centre stage once. Some, I've remained at until the small hours, but for the majority, I leave early. The few where I've stayed long after bedtime and enjoyed a delightful nightcap with the groom or a close family friend have generally been when there hasn't been a constant sense of rushing around, fretting or mild panic about unimportant details throughout the day.

For a wedding party to flourish, a majestic cake, delicious food, and a well-stocked open bar will start you off on the right track. Sometimes, little surprise quirks can work well: a singing waiter, a signature customised drink, a party trick or a secret raffle. The very best parties always contain an element of surprise. Be cognisant of your guest's needs. For example, charging stations for phones and even flip-flops for those strapped for hours in high heels. Ensure tissues, hand lotion, mints, chewing gum and mini body products are available in the restrooms. Small details like this make a big impression.

These days, there are so many types of weddings: reception-only, destination, micro (great for those on a budget) and green weddings that I'm never exactly sure what I've been invited to. Another complication is the matter of wedding gifts. I believe that if I'm asked to a wedding – whether I attend or not – I should give a gift. I've received many wedding invitations that say 'gifts are not expected' only to arrive at the venue to a table full of gifts. I went to one recently, and upon leaving, I was handed a small, personalised gift as a mark of gratitude for attending, in addition to the standard wedding favours left on our table. It was called an 'exit bag', which I thought was a nice touch.

You can guarantee that most weddings will last for hours, regardless of reception or party. I've never understood why there isn't a chill-out/hang-out room at larger weddings for guests to relax away from the main venue. I often see guests sitting at their table, especially older guests, sometimes asleep or watching others dance. Most of the time, they look bored out of their minds. Offering a designated seating area for those guests who don't want to dance (sometimes for health reasons) makes all the more sense. Likewise, for reading material. I would recommend selected books, fiction and non-fiction, related to the location or history of the venue scattered around or left on tables for guests to skim through and ponder. This might sound strange, but it can elicit conversation instantly and be fun to read. Penguin's Little Black Classics, consisting of complete or extracts from books considered classics, are perfect for such occasions.

Similarly, I've noticed varying bar areas outside the main reception area, which guests love, including a cigar bar, calorific sundae bar, temperance bar and tapas (or taco) bar. The temperance bar I experienced recently focused specifically on kombucha drinks and was a delight. Games like Jenga or Bocce can work well externally, as can temporarily hired Photo Booths or arcade machines like pinball – although these are far more expensive. Trust me, even today, when I meet certain friends, I'm always reminded of that wedding with *The Addams Family* pinball machine, never mind who got married!

Bristol-based Home Leisure Direct are an excellent – and entertaining – company to check out for games room treats. I was also at a wedding recently where the groom hired an artist to draw caricatures of all the guests. She created a 'party wall' to display all the drawings until the night's end. It was quite a sight and ended up as a beautiful photograph. It was a lot of work for the artist to manage guests, explain the end result, and instruct them how to sit, but she handled it with aplomb. Only a few noble guests refused – their loss.

A crucial part of any wedding day is the reception. After a few drinks, every guest may think they are a natural-born orator – quite the opposite. Keep toasts short. Two minutes is long enough. Tasteful cut-offs are an art in themselves, and I have yet to see this expertly executed. It's never easy interrupting someone, but sometimes – for the benefit of the other guests' sanity – needs must.

Seating is important, but not the be-all and end-all. Don't try too hard to be the matchmaker. If there are guests who like each other, I can assure you they will eventually be introduced. I much rather enjoy seating people from different age groups and backgrounds together. This makes the conversation far more fun! The majority will group people with similar backgrounds and interests… boring and easy, I say.

I've always found that a personal touch can work wonders when it comes to music. For instance, find out the favourite bands or artists of a bridesmaid, father of the bride, or even someone less formally connected like the photographer, videographer, florist or caterer. Often forgotten, they'll appreciate the subtlety. Choose music that suits the location, venue and season of the wedding. Make sure the music is straightforward enough to dance to. Save the obscure Aaron Copland piece for another event. A great DJ will also take care of the lighting, a skill in itself, from ambient uplighting to setting the romantic mood to strobe and moving lights to set the disco alive.

Hiring a professional to organise the wedding reception can be much easier. Attempting to juggle everything yourself is lunacy. There are far more moving parts and details than you would expect. You are dealing with two 'sides', so to speak, two entire families. You need someone behind the scenes. Focus on ensuring your guests have a memorable day and delegate the nuts and bolts to an expert instead.

Ensure children have some entertainment, ideally in their own supervised room, so they don't get too bored. Keep the kids busy!

Chapter 14

The Office Party

"The annual Office Party starts along about noon on December 24 and ends two or three months later, depending on how long it takes the boss to find out who set fire to his wastebasket, threw the water cooler out of the window, and betrayed Miss O'Malley in the men's washroom."

Corey Ford

A fair proportion of more lavish parties have an underlying commercial purpose. They might be a book launch, a TV premiere, a film wrap, a restaurant opening or a fashion show. Their primary purpose is not to bring happiness but to promote a firm, product or place.

Of course, that is all fine – the attendees can still have a whale of a time, and at least the costs are covered by the business promoting. I have launched several clubs, bars and restaurants with a party to generate publicity. The guest list for such functions is somewhat different from a personal gathering. You need to invite journalists, influencers, celebrities and the like. The evening should create a buzz that grabs media attention. The rituals at such parties are somewhat different from private gatherings. For example, these days, there is something of an expectation that guests will receive a goody bag as they leave.

Of course, companies also throw parties for their staff: to celebrate great results, Christmas, going public, an office move, or a thousand other reasons. These functions can be great fun but tend to have a very particular atmosphere. In the modern age, the once-standard debauchery has all but disappeared.

Nowadays, romantic relationships between staff members are frowned upon or even forbidden. Drunkenness in front of work colleagues is seen as

103

wholly inappropriate, so the mood of these work parties has calmed down a lot. While this is a good thing, a part of me misses the scandalous goings-on, a regular feature of staff shindigs.

Despite the puritanism of today's workplace, corporate bashes remain big business. Be it hospitality at Lord's Cricket Ground, Wimbledon, Royal Ascot or Brands Hatch, hosting high-rollers is among the chief money spinners for many of these prestigious sporting fixtures.

Corporate events are fundamentally different from private parties. They are a business expense – usually for public relations purposes – so the budgets are typically much higher than if someone is paying the bill. While corporate affairs *are* social engagements, there is an underlying business purpose – rather than purely for fun. So inevitably, such functions will be more restrained in terms of the guests' behaviour, and guests will be networking for work rather than chatting for pleasure.

If you want to mix with captains of industry, the two best social events in the calendar are *The Sunday Times* Business Party at Claridge's and Monday evening at The Chelsea Flower Show. Most financiers and CEOs who matter are invited, and each event provides a wonderful display of power broking and tycoons at play. You can monitor who is in the ascendance and who has been cast into the outer wilderness by their presence or absence at such gatherings. I was persona non grata for a bit, but I seem to be back in good graces (with some, at least) these days.

Chapter 15

Surviving a Children's Party

As a father of three, I've experienced my fair share of birthday parties for children. I hate excessive and expensive children's parties with indulgent party bags. There is no need for this. They are no more than an ego trip for bored parents.

The best location is never your own home. Far better and free, a local park or farm (animal petting party), wildlife park, playground or back garden. Hiring a community centre or village hall is cheap enough if you book far enough in advance. That way, you don't have to bother so much with the cleaning up. Sports are another winner; mini golf is a hoot even for parents, ice skating, roller skating (ever so trendy now), rock climbing walls, or a good old-fashioned bowling alley.

Start the day with an incredible birthday breakfast. The best times to have a party are ones that fit around your child's usual eating times, so say 11am to 1pm or 3pm to 5pm. Avoid 'peak' hours. Late morning is perfect because you won't have to serve a full meal. The party should last no longer than 2-3 hours for a maximum of around 20-30 guests. Sunday is the best day by far, except on a holiday weekend. Children five years or younger should be accompanied by a parent or guardian.

For food, stick to simple classic fare like jelly and ice cream, jam or ham sandwiches, pick-and-mix sweets, crisps, crisps and more crisps, grapes, cucumber sticks and marshmallows.

For entertainment, cheap alternatives include face painting, temporary tattoos, scavenger hunts, treasure hunts, oversize Connect 4, garden chess, friendship bracelet-making station, mini-mazes and yard games. Buy paper tripod stands and use chalk and crayons. Have the children work as a team to make a large mural (perhaps made up of handprints and footprints) or a splatter paint concept idea on an old bedsheet. Have a story-themed party and encourage children to dress up as their favourite fictional characters. Have a special 'guest' offer a live reading! Superheroes always work, as do the inevitable Harry Potter parties (butterbeer, anyone?). Pirates, princesses and fairies are always loved. Try to bring these themes to life through decorations and costumes.

Consider timeless games like Duck Duck Goose, Pass the Parcel, Musical Chairs, Musical Bumps, Musical Statues, Charades, Hot Potato, Hula Hoop competition and Simon Says. Pin the Tail on the Donkey is also a hit. A 'giant bubble show' can be set up for just a few pounds (washing up liquid, hot water, glycerine and bubble wands) and can provide hours of fun. Making bath bombs or slime balls takes too much effort.

Dressing-up, costume, pyjama and sleepover (slumber) parties (think glow-in-the-dark props) all are good fun, but, inevitably, I find children need far more ways than one to be entertained. Some quirky ideas you can perform as a host include becoming a secret agent for the day or dressing up as a wizard or clown. Or be the supervisor of a 'supervised food fight' – I dare you. If you're fortunate enough to have your own outdoor wood-fired pizza oven, a DIY pizza party can work wonders, especially as it's a super easy way to care for everyone's taste and dietary restrictions. Lay out the various ingredients and toppings, have them roll and cut the dough, and let their masterpiece take shape. You never know, this could be the impetus for the next great pizza restaurateur!

I'm not a great fan of bouncy castles or trampolines – there are too many safety concerns. Same for any swimming pool event. I much prefer soft play centres, sandpits and adventure playgrounds, as do my children. Even better is movie night camping in the back garden. You only need a few cheap tents, a movie projector and a big white wall. Popcorn and soda under the stars: bliss. Can you sing? If so, how about a kids' karaoke? You could incorporate something like YouTube's 'Just Dance' for song and dance. Are you a magician? Learn a few quick card tricks, and children will be entranced. Ever tried a puppet show? It's not as difficult as it sounds, especially with the range of glove puppets on the market – safari animals are a particular highlight.

To save money you can share the party with other children whose birthday it is. This can create a drastic reduction in costs. Remember, if you think of a classroom of 30 students, you have a 70 per cent chance of two classmates sharing a birthday (within a few days of each other). Your child will be happy with anything, as they will have fun. It makes no difference to them if the party costs £50 or £5,000.

With every passing year and candle on the cake, a birthday party should be just as memorable for your child as it is for you. I have friends who barely even remember their own birthdays – what sort of example does that set? If you make an effort for your own birthday party, your children will copy your example and look forward to all the wonderful parties ahead.

Chapter 16

The Lost Art of the Party Piece

Simply put, a party piece is a poem, song, ballad, dance, medley, story, performance or trick someone performs to entertain others. There are examples of party pieces from as far back as diarist Samuel Pepys. Indeed, poet Samuel Taylor Coleridge's party piece was reciting his long narrative ballad, *Christabel*, while novelist D.H. Lawrence was rumoured to recite the poetry of A.C. Swinburne as his party piece. The art of the party piece has fallen out of fashion in recent years, although it remains an integral feature of parties in parts of Ireland, Scotland and Australia.

There is something special about the Irish, a nation of gifted talkers, writers and performers, and the party piece may even stem from their incredible pub culture – impromptu performances from fiddlers and storytellers are commonplace. In the past, travellers would pass through, regaling the locals with stories in return for a bowl of stew or a pint. The excellent film *Michael Collins* by Irish director Neil Jordan features many evocative party pieces. Fast forward to modern times, and it was interesting to hear on a recent podcast by Adam Buxton, Hollywood actor – and recent author – Tom Hanks mention his staple party piece as being the hit country song the *Green, Green Grass of Home*.

More raucous party pieces might be a striptease or a passionate tango. Certain characters like to perform a comedy routine or tell a favourite anecdote. The academic Alan Warren Friedman defined the party piece as 'a peculiar kind of public self-representation'. I've always liked this phrase. Party pieces are not formal recitals. Instead, the best are spontaneous and reminiscent of the theme and atmosphere of the party. They act as an oral bridge. I can only ever remember party pieces performed at my father's many parties forty-odd years ago. Generally, it would be a short verse from a poem or play delivered in a burst that stopped everyone in their tracks. Even the hardiest journalists and literary critics – mainstay guests at these parties – were roused with emotion from such open displays. Nowadays, I guess the only way you might hear one is to come to one of my parties!

Chapter 17

No Frills Partying

Many first-time hosts think throwing a party must be an expensive, elaborate event. Not true! You can find venues that won't charge any rental if enough drinks are sold. In those circumstances, you do have to warn guests that there will be a cash bar. Or you can hold a soiree at home and suggest guests bring a bottle or nibbles. Students are usually on very tight budgets, yet they throw parties almost every night of the week. All you need to make the night go with a swing is a crowd of guests determined to get on down and a minimum amount of preparation.

With careful planning and creativity, you can throw a fantastic party without breaking the bank. Some of the best parties I've been to have been put together at the last minute on a shoestring budget. Who knows what the night can bring if you keep an open mind? The most essential factor about hosting a great party is that the guests come!

The key to hosting a budget-friendly party is prioritising what's most important to you and your guests and being creative in finding cost-effective solutions. Choosing a theme, no matter how small, can make your party more exciting and focused. Being extra focused will also help you watch your wallet. It can also help you decide about decorations, food and activities that fit your budget. If money is tight, it doesn't mean you have to compromise on fun or the quality of the party. With some planning and creativity, you can host a memorable and enjoyable party without extravagant spending. Here are some tips to help you save:

Set a Budget:
- Determine how much you can afford to spend on the party. Be realistic and stick to this budget.

Plan Ahead:

- Start planning well in advance to give yourself time to get organised and find the best deals and offers.

Venue:

- Host the party at your own home or a friend's house to save on venue hire costs. Consider free outdoor locations like parks, beaches or community centres, which are often more affordable and accessible than renting event spaces. However, make sure your space can comfortably accommodate your guest list.

Guest List:

- Keep the guest list manageable. Fewer guests mean less food, drinks, and party supplies.

Invitations:

- Send digital invitations via email or social media using free online design tools to save on printing and postage costs.

Music:

- Create a playlist in advance instead of hiring a DJ or live band.

Games and Entertainment:

- Organise fun and budget-friendly games or activities like charades, board games, or outdoor games like Cornhole to keep your guests entertained.

DIY Decorations:

- Create decorations using inexpensive materials like paper, balloons and streamers. Consider a theme that allows you to repurpose items you already have at home.

Food:

- Stick to budget-friendly simple dishes like finger foods, dips and pasta salads. These are staple crowd-pleasers. Think about asking guests to bring a dish to share, pot-luck style. Shop at Aldi or Lidl for snacks – no one can tell the difference at a party between their crisps or crudités and those from their costlier rivals.

Drink:

- Serve inexpensive drinks like homemade iced tea, lemonade or a signature punch.

Bring Your Own Bottle: if you plan to serve alcohol, ask guests to bring drinks to share. Use a wallpaper table as a makeshift bar.

DIY entertainment:
- Create a playlist instead of hiring a DJ or live band. Organise simple games or activities that don't require expensive equipment.

Borrow or Rent:
- If you need extra tables, chairs, or decorations, consider borrowing or renting them rather than buying. Spread the word.

Use Coupons and Discounts:
- Look out for cashback offers when purchasing supplies and groceries. Look for deals when shopping for party supplies, food, and decorations. Buying in bulk can also save you money. Try charity shops and car boot sales.

Minimalist Tableware:
- Use reusable or disposable tableware and utensils to save on cleanup time and expenses.

Cleanup:
- Enlist the help of friends or family members to assist with cleanup after the party. Consider using eco-friendly, reusable or recyclable party supplies to minimise waste.

Chapter 18

Party Killers

"Like other parties of the kind, it was first silent, then talky, then argumentative, then disputatious, then unintelligible, then altogether, then inarticulate, and then drunk. When we had reached the last step of this glorious ladder, it was difficult to get down again without stumbling."

Lord Byron

A party is a fragile thing; it doesn't take too much to destroy the occasion. Some of these might be external influences – rain on a garden party, for example, or a disastrous date clash with another popular event like a major sporting fixture.

But there also lurk dangers within: ill-mannered guests who can ruin a delightful gathering. These beasts come in various stripes:

- Snobs: these are the types who are always critical and see any social get-together as an excuse to complain that the guests are déclassé, or the food is mediocre, or the drinks are too naff, or the music is too loud, or the venue is all wrong. They asphyxiate the mood and hate to see anyone having a fun time. They are usually motivated by envy and are too lazy or mean to host a party according to their stratospheric standards. If they moan too much, then encourage them to find somewhere else which would suit them better – and make sure never to invite them anywhere else again!

- Drunks: we are all sober until we have drunk too much alcohol – after that, we are generally much worse company. Intelligent and well-behaved guests know their limits and restrain their consumption of intoxicating beverages. Unfortunately, some have a problem with alcohol – and a few, very occasionally, lose control and binge. They all need help, but once they are much the worse for wear, some can become unreasonable and offensive. If a partner accompanies them, then it makes sense to enlist their other half to get them to calm down.

Ultimately, if they are an aggressive drunk, the best solution is to encourage them to head home (never behind the wheel). This is a delicate matter and requires finesse from the host. At events where there are door attendants, recruiting them to assist in coaxing the inebriated guest to depart makes sense. To a certain degree, every host who serves booze at a party has facilitated this state of affairs, so a brutal approach to a sloshed guest is never justified. Better an understanding but firm attitude, especially if there have been complaints from other guests about the drunk's 'exuberant' antics. Most of us have been there, after all. I can recall the first time I got genuinely hammered at a party at university. I drank pints of Pimm's as if it were fruit juice and ended up sitting down with my trousers around my ankles – and vomit down my front. I had to be gently escorted to my room by loyal friends. Not a very edifying spectacle but a rite of passage, I suppose.

- Bores: These are an insidious breed who sneak up while the host is unaware. They drone on and send other guests into deep comas. In a way, they represent the opposite extreme to drunks: rather than cranking up the excitement to excessive levels, they suffocate it – but alienate your guests nonetheless. Screening out bores is a challenge – frequently, they are spouses of friends, the old pal who has fossilised, or the tedious relative who must be invited to the wedding reception for family reasons. You cannot legitimately eject a guest for being boring; the best remedy is to gather them all together so they can bore the pants off each other. God forbid anyone gets stuck on their table!

- Gatecrashers: I had a shattering experience early on in my hosting career. I held a party at home when I was about seventeen, and my parents were away, and gatecrashers stole my mum's jewellery. So, I have always been acutely aware of the threat such interlopers can present to friendly festivities. I suppose there are two sorts of gatecrashers: genuine friends of friends who can be authentically vouched for and complete strangers who have no legitimate connection to the event.

The latter category must *always* be excluded. Whether you welcome the former is at your discretion: treating them as a new friend is the generous act. But it depends on capacity; if you feel such an uninvited guest would fit in and can be trusted. My advice is to treat every incident on a case-by-case basis and use your judgment. You should never feel obliged to let anyone in if you have not been warned of their presence.

The parties I host only encourage legal intoxicants like beer and wine. Guests who take drugs are committing an offence and frequently tilt the atmosphere of a party to the wilder side. Drug-taking involves drug dealers and other unsavoury characters, and my preference is to avoid the whole scene.

Chapter 19

All Tomorrow's Parties

"The key to a good party is filling a room with guests more interesting than you."

Steve Rubell

My eye was caught recently by an excellent article in *Business Insider* entitled 'The Gatsby of Silicon Alley' by Darius Rafieyan. It chronicles the tales of a young Silicon Valley whiz named Andrew Yeung, whose parties have struck a chord with young creatives dying for human connection post-COVID. He now has a sprawling events empire. I like his style. He started a party called Junto – an invite-only party named after a secret society founded by Benjamin Franklin. You should read about him, follow his lead and perhaps when you're in New York next, you can attend one of his 'free' parties and let me know what all the fuss is about.

He reminds me a little of the late and great Jim Haynes, who hosted an open-house party for decades every Sunday night at his apartment in Paris. I attended more than once – as did Graeme – and was always warmly welcomed and entertained. His routine was an astonishing and generous act. He offered an open door and food and drink to complete strangers who showed up at his Paris pad. There was a nominal charge to defray the costs.

It is estimated that in the 30-odd years that Jim was hosting his Sunday evening open house, over 100,000 guests enjoyed his hospitality. You turned up, and a completely unpredictable selection of locals, ex-pats, and tourists filled the room. It was always a hugely life-affirming evening. Jim wrote several memoirs, including *Thanks for Coming!* which is out of print but available second-hand. Jim, if I may say so, was quite the peripatetic maverick himself, and we both shared a love of the theatre and the magnificent city of Edinburgh.

I've also been reading about the re-emergence of 'salons', particularly in America. Sunday Salon, Salon Surprise… the global trend is fast upon us. Salons flourished in France throughout the 17th and 18th centuries; they were essentially gatherings for exchanging ideas. More recently, the legendary Theodora di Marco and her twin Norma hosted weekly infamous soirée salons at 10 Pembroke Road in Notting Hill throughout much of the 1980s.

Later, 'Beckett's' was hosted by the charismatically troubled Beckett Rosset in the West Village. At the last time of checking, 'Beckett's' was either closing, closed or abandoned. Regardless, it is/was an outlet for dozens of young writers, critics, artists, theatre actors and filmmakers to party – a glorified speakeasy, a modern Warhol Factory.

The queen of salons appears to be Susan MacTavish Best, who runs Salon Host (www.thesalonhost.com), a resource designed to inspire others to host community events. She has a posthoc (www.posthoc.com) business that organises events in Soho, New York City and the Arts District in LA, as well as in London and Washington. She believes real-life get-togethers are more critical than ever in the smartphone age, providing conversation, intellectual stimulation and human connection – in person. She says meeting new people and listening and learning are vital to building and sustaining communities. I completely agree with her. The salon world is appealing, a gathering of sorts, not just a party, more than a nightclub, much more than an open mic or get-together. If any readers have any ideas for a salon in London, please reach out. I'll fund the venue if you can create the inspiration and host.

Another world-class host is my friend Brent Hoberman. He created the Founders Forum in 2005, and I have attended this high-powered symposium every year since. It now takes place in Britain, the US and various other countries. It brings together hundreds of tech and media entrepreneurs, investors, politicians and other movers and shakers for an annual conference about the state of business, innovation and the world. Brent always throws a fabulous opening night party, typically somewhere spectacular like The Orangery at Kensington Palace. The evening is always a fantastic piece of curation and hospitality.

I'm not sure what the future of parties will offer. I try to live in the now rather than the past or the future. Who knows? There may be another pandemic, and we'll wish we had had more parties in the meantime. Or maybe the new daft craze of virtual parties (perhaps not so new anymore) will prosper with the advent of Artificial Intelligence and the Metaverse bandwagon. All I can say is I'm glad I'm not part of that generation. I'd be happy never to hear the words Zoom, Teams or FaceTime again.

The most memorable parties I've hosted have been those where I've been an active participant rather than an onlooker. So, become involved and have your guests involved. There's no such thing as a perfect host, but you can be a memorable one.

Chapter 20

The Death of the Party?

An article appeared in *The New York Times* in 2015 entitled, The Death of the Party. It described how twenty and thirty-somethings were not hosting house parties like previous generations. It offered various explanations for why inviting friends around for food, drink and dancing was falling out of fashion. It suggested that the young people live in smaller homes that are more geographically dispersed than in the past, more complicated for guests to reach. It described how hosts worried about how foodie culture meant guests were more challenging to satisfy when it came to culinary offerings. By contrast, I can recall from my university days that no one bothered providing anything to eat – it was all about drinking and meeting the opposite sex. The article said that students were studying too hard and were too broke to have the time or money to throw parties.

The article also highlighted how many Millennials and Gen Z now initiate relationships online, thanks to apps like Tinder, Bumble and Hinge. The digital era means finding romance mostly happens via a smartphone, not at a cocktail or supper party. Much research suggests this works for the most eligible 20 per cent of the population but not for the majority. I think the answer is for more of those in the 18-30 age groups to copy their parents and throw parties – and make new friends IRL (in real life), as they say.

Part of my motivation in writing this book was to encourage the generations after me to continue organising social gatherings. One of the side effects of lockdowns during 2020/21 was to stifle conventional socialising. It turbocharged an unhealthy dependence on smartphones and exacerbated introverted habits among too many younger people. Parties were essentially banned for two years, and so many of those who would regularly invite friends around got out of the habit and gave up. Similarly, people became lazy and even scared about going out – it was so much easier to slump at home watching streamed movies while scrolling on your smartphone.

But this is not a genuine life! Virtual communications don't compare to the real thing. Judging potential dates based purely on their image on a dating app means you exclude a considerable proportion of possible partners – it discounts vital aspects like personality, sense of humour, empathy and so many other important characteristics. It might appear efficient, but it eliminates the magical power of serendipity – being introduced to the friend of a friend whom you would never have connected with online.

And, of course, parties are about far more than prospective romantic involvements. They are about making new platonic friendships and nurturing existing ones. They might even be about making valuable contacts for work or a hobby. Of course, the latter might be possible via LinkedIn. But how much better to come across a prospective client/supplier/business partner/investor/recruit at a social affair and share a joke or two before discussing business? Then you will surely have a better idea if you can trust and work with them.

Bibliography

Articles

Blackwell, E. (2015) Entertaining at home – only better; Looking to host a special event with a personal touch? Throw a party at someone else's house. Crain's Chicago business. Vol. 38 (46),

Campos, S. (2019) Vegan? Paleo? Gluten-Free?! How to Throw a Hollywood Dinner Party to Please All Guests. *Hollywood Reporter*. 42560–61.

Dunn, J. (2018) throw a party with heart. Vol. 19. New York: Time Incorporated.

Friedman, A. W. (1999) Party Pieces in Joyce's *Dubliners*. James Joyce quarterly. 36 (3), 471–484.

Gibbons, D. (2002) How to throw the perfect party. Vol. 9. New York: IAC.

Lieberman, S. (2017) How to Throw a Relaxed Parisian Dinner Party. *New York Times*.

Rafieyan, D. (2023) The Gatsby of Silicon Alley: Meet the 27-year-old Google employee who's throwing tech's hottest parties. *Business Insider*.

Zacher, H. (2023) The company Christmas party and employee happiness. *Scientific reports*. 13 (1), 337–337.

Books

Bee, Jaymz and Gregor, Jan (1997) *Cocktail Parties for Dummies*, IDG Books, California.

Blaikie, Thomas (2005) *Blaikie's Guide to Modern Manners*, Fourth Estate, London.

Bratchpiece, D. and Innes, K. (2021) *Brickwork: A Biography of The Arches.* Salamander Street Ltd.

Clayton, Nicholas (2016) *A Butler's Guide to Entertaining.* London, Batsford.

Davis, D. (2006) *Party of the century: the fabulous story of Truman Capote and his black and white ball.* Hoboken, N.J: John Wiley.

Debrett's Guide to Hosting and Entertaining (2020) London, Debrett's Ltd.

Draper, Dorothy (1941) *Entertaining is Fun!* Doubleday, New York.

Esquire's Handbook for Hosts, (1977) Hearst Communications, NY.

Field, Suzette (2012) *A Curious Invitation.* Picador, London

Gagliano, R. (2017) *Brunch is Hell: How to Save the World by Throwing a Dinner Party.* Little, Brown US.

Grey, Nick (2022) *The 2-Hour Cocktail Party.* Lioncrest, US.

Johnston, Susanna (1994) *Parties – A Literary Companion.* Macmillan, London.

Knowles, E. (2014) The Oxford Dictionary of Quotations. OUP, Oxford.

MacPherson, Charles (2013) *The Butler Speaks.* Random House, USA.

Parker, P. (2018) *The art of gathering: how we meet and why it matters.* New York: Riverhead Books.

Pritchard, Mari (1981) *Guests & Hosts.* OUP, Oxford.

Rey, J (2013) *How to Dine in Style,* The Bodleian Library, Oxford.

Robertson, M. (2018) *The Cocktail Bible.* Octopus Publishing Group Ltd.

Van Wyck, Bronson (2019) *Born to Party, Forced to Work.* Phaidon Press, London

Vivaldo, Denise (2009) *The Entertaining Encyclopaedia.* Robert Rose Inc, Toronto.

The Oxford Dictionary of Quotations

Podcast

The Adam Buxton Podcast. April 18th, 2023. Episode 201, Tom Hanks. Available at https://podcasts.apple.com/gb/podcast/the-adam-buxton-podcast/id1040481893?i=1000612817215

Graeme Boyd (l) and Luke Johnson (r) at Honest Jon's Records, London, May 2024. Photo uncredited.

Authors

Luke Johnson has been an entrepreneur for over four decades. He is a director and part-owner of the bakery chain GAIL's, and was previously chairman of PizzaExpress and Channel 4 Television. He is chairman of Brighton Pier Group PLC and a director/part-owner at Brompton Bicycles. He has written six previous books and wrote a weekly column for 20 years in successively *The Sunday Telegraph, The Financial Times and The Sunday Times.* He has owned multiple party venues for many years and has thrown too many parties to remember. www.lukejohnson.org

Graeme Boyd is a Chartered Librarian who previously managed the archives of Greenpeace International in Amsterdam and Condé Nast in London. He was the Learning Resource Specialist at Berlin Brandenburg International School and Head Librarian at St. Francis College in São Paulo. Graeme is a consultant for UNESCO's Institute for Lifelong Learning, Workshop Facilitator and Programme Leader for the International Baccalaureate and Evaluation Team member for the Council of International Schools. He has worked as a consultant to Luke Johnson since 2014. He is a Fellow of the Royal Society of Arts. www.graemeboyd.com

Contributor

Peter York is an author, journalist, broadcaster and management consultant. He started his writing career as Style Editor at Harper's & Queen magazine and, over the last 40 years, has written 12 books and numerous articles. He has contributed to television programmes from Newsnight to The Tube. His latest book, *The War Against the BBC*, is co-authored by Professor Patrick Barwise. He is a former President of The Media Society. His new podcast, Peter York's Culture Wars House Party, starts in June 2024.

Recipes Disclaimer

We are not responsible for the outcome of any recipe you try from this book. You may not achieve the results desired due to variations in ingredients, cooking temperatures, typos, errors, omissions, or individual cooking ability. You should always use your best judgement when cooking with raw ingredients such as eggs, chicken or fish and seek expert advice before beginning if you are unsure. You should always take care not to injure yourself or others on sharp knives or other cooking implements or to burn yourself or others while cooking. You should examine the contents of ingredients prior to preparation and consumption of these recipes to be fully aware of and to accurately advise others of the presence of substances which might provoke an adverse reaction in some consumers. Recipes available in this book may not been formally tested by us or for us and we do not provide any assurances nor accept any responsibility or liability with regard to their originality, efficacy, quality or safety.

This book and its contents are the property of Luke Johnson, except where certain rights are stated as being limited or qualified and attributed to other parties or persons.